THE SUNDAY EXPRESS
UP COUNTRY YEARBOOK

THE SUNDAY EXPRESS
UP COUNTRY YEARBOOK

THURLOW CRAIG

Illustrations by
Bill Martin

ARTHUR BARKER LIMITED   LONDON
A subsidiary of Weidenfeld (Publishers) Limited

Contents

Author's Note

The stories about animals and birds in this book are all true. They did not take place in one year or on the same farm and some go back to the early years of this century – but the majority of them happened at our farm Pantffynnonlas during the last three years.

T.C.

For Ann
with all my love

January

We Move into our Cottage

We both felt that the caravan in which we have been living for the last seven weeks was not the place in which to celebrate the New Year.

So we made preparations to welcome it in the cottage living-room, one wall of which has now been panelled with knotty pine. On the other side of the room is a gorgeous old Coalbrook-dale kitchen range with a massive stone surround standing out sixteen inches from the thick stone wall. It must weigh several tons and the idea is that after a fire has been burning for several days, the absorbed heat is slowly and constantly given out.

Most of our furniture is in the stables but our big bookcase, which occupies one wall and is tremendously heavy, is already in place.

For the rest, after a blazing fire had been lit, we moved a couple of chairs in for us and my workroom table for the television drinks, not forgetting a Christmas centrepiece that my wife had made in the caravan. There was also a big rug in front of the fire for the animals and there they all were: four cats, Gretchen the Dobermann, and Meg the Rottweiler pup, lying in a compact mass and simply loving it.

I am certain that they felt exactly as we did; the little house was welcoming us all with open arms. There was an extraordinary feeling of warmth. Indeed, more than once we had to move our chairs further from the roaring fire and the little battery television set was giving a far better picture than it ever did in the caravan.

I looked at the thermometer and to my amazement saw that the temperature was only just above 10°C.; yet we were all as warm as could be. The temperature in the caravan would have seemed murderously cold.

Came midnight and out I went to welcome the New Year in, bringing in a lump of coal and a piece of bread. Having put out food for the animals in their respective bowls (with some misgivings, since they had never fed all together before), we drank to the New Year. It was strange to see cats and dogs eating together with no thought of poaching. But obviously they were loving every moment of it. So were we: it was vastly different to what might have been in the caravan.

Before going to bed (in the caravan) we had a discussion. Many years had passed since anyone had lived in the cottage – let alone celebrated a New Year in it – and we were sick of that caravan.

Next day we put our first New Year resolution into effect. We set a bed up in the living-room.

Soon all the clothes we had in the caravan were strung along lines to air. They were wringing wet from condensation. When dry, they were folded up and accommodated in the bookcase. The same piece of furniture also accommodated the various little ornaments from the caravan, necessary cutlery, my shaving gear, and so forth – and there was plenty of blessed room in which to move around. We were both by now in an advanced state of caravan claustrophobia.

Heating and cooking would be taken care of by the old range; a pressure lamp would supply ample lighting. It may be months before we can use the top rooms, as they have to be re-ceilinged and materials are scarce; but no matter, the little house will be lived in.

And the first day we had installed ourselves, our robin popped in through a broken pane to demand breakfast. So here we are, my wife Ann, myself, and the animals, all as happy as grigs. And I forgot to add that our grig – or cricket-on-the-hearth – was chirping away gaily as we welcomed in the New Year.

'For whither thou goest, I will go; and where thou lodgest I will lodge; thy people shall be my people, and thy God my God: where thou diest, will I die, and there will I be buried: the Lord do so to me and more also, if ought but death part thee and me.'

Written over three thousand years ago, that sentence from the Book of Ruth is my favourite in all the Bible. In my mind, it emphasizes the greatest characteristic of human belief: that of utter loyalty to those whom you love.

It may be thought strange that I should choose such a verse to introduce a very small donkey, Ann's latest acquisition, called Rebecca. And yet, is it so strange? The ass looms large and dignified in both the Old and the New Testaments. It looms large in my book too.

Over six years ago we sold the big farm and bought a very small smallholding. This meant selling most of the stock. We sold nearly all the horses at a loss to people we knew would look after them, giving two of the best to a young couple getting married. We were left with two, one of whom was a wanderer. That is why we bought Rebecca.

Quietly, without any ostentation, she would keep them under control, even though she was only two years old. When we bought her she had never seen or tasted the contents of a horse-bucket. She had never been under a roof, in a horse-trailer, or had a halter on her pretty head.

But she survived it all with the sense of a donkey – and don't ever believe that a donkey is stupid. They are far more intelligent than horses, which is why horses always revere and follow them. The only thing they like is to take their time and fit the facts to their own gait.

Rebecca arrived and was put into the spare loose box, which at first she didn't like at all. I put in a nice bucket of cold well-water and she ignored it. I then put in a small half-bucket of bran, oats and watered cow-treacle, well mixed, but she wouldn't look at that until I picked up a sticky handful and rubbed it on her nose. From then on she began to like me, until Ann came home from her shopping. Then and there she transferred her love and that is how it is now.

She regards me as Roger the Lodger, a useful encumbrance in case of dire necessity. That is where my text from the first chapter of the Book of Ruth comes in: Rebecca follows my wife around like a familiar spirit. Whither she goes, Rebecca will go too. I get the impression that although I wanted a donkey to look after the horses, Rebecca seems to think that her task in life is to look after Ann. So be it.

When the rains come and Ann gets bogged down to the middle when going down to the water-pump, Rebecca will pull her out and I won't have to bother. If it is too great a task, she'll bray for me.

When she first came I had to teach her how to bray because all she could manage was a high squeak. Another rather lovely point is that when she arrived she was dressed like a mammoth, with hair ten inches long all over. Now that Ann has groomed that off, she's neat and tidy – but more than that, she has the well-defined Cross of Jesus over her shoulders and down her back.

*Patchy
Makes a
Strange Find*

The name of our new farm is Pantffynnonlas, which translated into English means 'the Blue Well in the Hollow'. We were told that the blue well had long since been sold to a neighbouring farmer, who very kindly told us that we could tap it whenever we liked. He never used it himself.

Since coming to live here we have had to bring up all our water from another neighbour every day in five-gallon cans by

Land Rover, and occasionally we run short. Ann at one time discovered a new spring, with which we hoped to provide a constant water supply for house and farm, but since then that spring, like many others hereabouts, showed signs of drying up in rainless spells. We would have to find another answer to our water problem.

The other morning my wife and I went out to feed the horses their corn, because in this fine weather they spend their nights outside.

Patchy, her skewbald roan, came up soaked in mud to the elbows, and we wondered where, in this drought, he had done it. However, it was easy to track the horses down to where they had discovered what might be an unsuspected bog or even a still-running spring. And so we did.

Down at the north-east corner, almost hidden by overgrowing grass, was a small well, which the previous owners of the farm had never even suspected. They were not farmers, had only used the place as a summer holiday residence, and had never repaired a fence or anything else on the place. Now we were thankful that none of their children had stumbled on this well, for it was over three feet deep, with steep sides and much overgrowing grass.

I returned to the house to bring down spade and brushing-hook, with which we got to work to see exactly what we had found. When we had done so we came to the conclusion that this was indeed 'the Blue Well in the Hollow' mentioned in the original deeds. There is a faint blue tint in the water, almost certainly due to copper sulphate, which makes it none the worse for drinking.

We cleaned it up and decided to brick it in, cover it, and install a small motor-pump to bring the water up to the farm. The commodity both Ann and I most missed, since we came to live here, was a constant supply of running water.

Then we heard a gentle nicker and looked up. Patchy was there behind us, coming to see what we were doing with the well he had discovered.

'Shove off, Catsmeat,' I said (he answers to both names). 'It's a bit slippery.'

But I had spoken too late. He slipped. In went his forelegs up to the neck, his hindquarters remaining on dry land. Looking helplessly at us he pleaded, *please get me out*, and, going back to the house for a rope, we did so. The beauty of the Welsh cob is that when in a jam they never panic, but help you all they can to get them out of trouble.

The horses will be kept out of that paddock until we get the well cemented.

A Narrow Escape for Two Bunnies

As we were still in the throes of building a hay-bay, septic tank and cementing in the well with a little motor-pump on it to provide water for the house – not to mention cementing the forecourt – there was masses of gravel, chippings and sand outside the drive gate.

Some time ago our neighbour who was making the hay-bay came to the cottage with two very small rabbits, one in each hand.

'Lucky that I didn't cut their little heads off,' he said. 'I was loading the field car with chippings when lo and behold up they came from the bottom of the pile on the spade. It seems that there must have been a bolt-hole from their burrow exactly where the gravel was dumped. It's half full of gravel now and I don't know how they got that far up.'

I examined both little rabbits. Their eyes were wide open and gazed into mine utterly without fear. They were fully furred and when I put them on the living-room floor they hopped about quite unperturbed, even when Gretchen and Meg lazily got up to investigate, sniffing them.

Ann put down a lettuce leaf which in no way interested them; they were obviously on a milk diet. But they hopped about very actively and just as obviously were at the age when they had not yet developed any sense of danger.

We returned them to the bolt-hole, popped them into it after scooping out enough gravel for them to get home.

We did not put any gravel over it, because a bolt-hole is

always useful to a rabbit in case a marauding polecat comes searching through the main entrance, which was at the base of a low stone wall about five yards away. But I cut a clod of turf and put that over the bolt-hole so that if danger arose Mrs Rabbit would be able to push it aside and get clear. My feeling was that if the mother had any sense she would remove her family to another place.

All wild things fear the smell of human beings just as much as they fear the smell of foxes, polecats and so on. These little rabbits had both been handled by our neighbour, Ann and myself. To their mother they might stink of danger and if she left the hole with the rest of her family, she would abandon them.

There was nothing to do but wait and see.

The next day I got up a little earlier than usual and for a time watched both holes from a discreet distance. There was no action there, so I made my way over the stone wall to where there is a very thick tangle of blackberry bushes. They were all out on the grass, four little ones playing around a big doe, who was busily filling herself with dewy grass.

Before myxomatosis practically eliminated the rabbit population, litters of eight and even more were common, but since they began to breed again, at least in the hills, two points are very obvious: most of them are brushwood rabbits and do not live in burrows, and the families are much smaller, averaging from two to four. So obviously the whole family was here.

Then – I must have left the cottage door ajar – Meg got into the act. She ambled up silently from behind, nudged me on the knee and went on to investigate the family.

Immediately the doe stamped her hind feet loudly on the ground in the traditional alarm signal of the rabbit tribe. She ran into the brush, followed by two of her children. But two of them remained playing unconcernedly and allowed Meg to get within sniffing distance.

I got up, walked forward and quietly shooed them into the thicket where the others had entered. Meg didn't understand why, but I felt that if they turned up at home two days running smelling of dogs and human beings, the mother might abandon them, and they were too young for that.

In they went, Meg and I returning to the house. Late that evening just before dark I went out, making sure that Meg wasn't with me. And there they were, so all was well.

Ann has often suggested changing the name of this farm from 'the Blue Well in the Hollow' to 'the Mucky Bog in the Marsh' and there is something in this. It seems to have rained or snowed nearly every day since last summer.

The only solid spot in the whole place is the concrete forecourt in front of the house, forty yards long by five to six yards wide. If you think that's long for a house, you're right, for that is what this type of farm is called. The longhouse style consists of a house at one end, then a couple of shippons or cow-houses, a calf-rearing pen, plus a brace of loose boxes for the working cobs, all in one building.

Today you are not allowed to build such an agglomeration because it is considered unhygienic to have the muck-heap within ten yards of the front door. Ours, across the forecourt, certainly doesn't qualify by present-day standards, but as this longhouse was built in 1720 it has been allowed to remain.

Three days we had a hard frost without snow and my heart sank, on looking out of the window, to see the Land Rover sitting on the forecourt with no anti-freeze in the radiator; she had been drained the previous day during one of our very rare warmer spells. I rushed out and started her up – and all was well.

During breakfast we saw two pied wagtails taking a walk around on the bonnet of the Land Rover. I remembered what my father had told me many years ago: birds that hop have one-sided brains, but birds which walk have both sides of their brain in working order. I don't know if there is any truth in this – possibly not – but I believe that the wagtails are our smallest walking birds. In any case they are fascinating little birds and take little notice of us when we go quite near them.

Having finished our breakfast I said that, in case of greater cold, I would put the Land Rover in the garage which has been built on to the south end of the house.

As I opened the door those two little birds flew off the bonnet, alighting on the forecourt. An hour previously I had again drained the radiator of cold water, which had frozen over into a hard film of ice. The wagtails landed on it and literally skated down it – apparently perfectly calm. It was the funniest sight I have seen for some time. At the bottom there was a long twist of hay across the slide and I expected a tumble with bated breath.

They twisted slightly as they skated down the eight-foot slide and I wondered what would happen when they reached it. Would they come to grief like the immortal Mr Pickwick when he went through the ice at Dingley Dell?

I needn't have worried. It seemed that they were not half an inch from that dangerous hay barrier when they took to their wings, swerved to the left and came down on hard, dry concrete without a skid about ten feet away, at the tail end of the Land Rover.

Here there were several handfuls of crushed oats, and as the wagtails pecked happily away I was puzzled. The books say that wagtails live on small flying or grounded insects, but at this time of year most insects disappear. I've often seen wagtails on our drystone wall where we feed the birds but there again the food generally contains a certain amount of meat or gravy. Do they eat grains of crushed oats or are there oatmeal insects still about?

*A Missel
Singing in a Gale*

Last Tuesday there were gale-to-storm-force warnings pretty well all round the country and, being barely fifteen miles from the Welsh coast, we got the full force plus torrential rain. But we were snug and warm in the cottage.

At ten o'clock in the morning we were still burning lights

because it was very dark, but at about the same time the rain stopped, and I took our narrow rabbit-spade (more commonly known nowadays as a trenching-tool) to ease the torrent that was pouring down the drive. The drive-entry lies at the bottom of two hills. In heavy rain all the ditches overflow and we have a roaring flood.

So there was I, bending to the wind and working away when my wife, well wrapped up, came out to give me a stand easy.

I sat on a big stone (bed-rock is very near the surface here) when suddenly my wife stood up listening and then pointed.

I looked up and there on the topmost branch of a leafless tree facing the gale, which was running at over 60 mph, stood a huge missel-thrush, singing at the top of his voice. For this reason – it is a habit with the species – they are sometimes known as storm-cocks.

He is by far the largest of all the thrush family, averaging eleven inches overall. He is native to this country and is often mistaken for another thrush, the fieldfare. Nowadays he is rather scarce, and it is quite an event to find one singing high up on an exposed tree in a howling gale.

There are two ways of spelling his name, either mistle or missel, and sometimes there are quite hot arguments about which it should be. Mistle is probably the commoner. Those who prefer mistle say that it is because he eats mistletoe, but I don't believe he does. I don't know any bird that eats mistletoe berries, which I was brought up to regard as poisonous. I prefer missel because it is an old Anglo-Saxon word meaning big – and that is exactly what he is, the largest of all the twelve members of the thrush family. But the authorities are agreed on one point: he is the only professional vocalist who does not mind the roughest weather – in fact, actually prefers it. All the other singers with reputations to maintain are most particular about the conditions in which they perform.

The missels, as I said, are rather scarce nowadays as are their cousins the song-thrushes that used to be so common.

We must have been watching and listening to this big storm-cock for at least ten minutes when down the road came Danny the Wood with a big load of logs for us.

This was a coincidence, as we had just been saying that as soon as we got rid of the water we'd have to go down to the town and order more logs because we had just burned the last

one. Then suddenly there was Danny kicking up huge splashes
on either side as the van ploughed through over a foot of water.

The bird flew away indignantly and we went to help Danny
unload. But before we were half finished he was back again,
taking up his song and vying with the gale which roared on
unabated.

We debated whether to put out a plate of mince, for missel-
thrushes prefer meat (in the form of grubs and all the insects
that other thrushes eat). But at this time of year such delicacies
as grubs are very scarce. So the birds have had to turn to berries
– and of these there were still plenty – particularly rowan or
mountain ash.

And obviously, as he was able to sing so well in such conditions, he must have been well fed and in fine fettle.

*A Frozen
Blackbird*

Sparrows and tits are very hardy little birds, mainly, I believe,
because of their sleeping habits.

Tits tend to congregate in a hole between the stones of a house
or wall, particularly in drystone walls. There, five or sometimes
more, they huddle together during the bitter nights and
manage to keep warm enough until the following day.

Much the same are the sparrows, nesting crowded under the
eaves where at least it is dry.

Some other birds are not so happy. When going out in the
mornings it is sometimes a good thing to inspect nearby shrubs
to see if there are any birds too cold and stiff to fly down when
their food is put out.

Another thing we always watch for, here in the hills during
hard weather, is an invasion of carrion crows and magpies.
When I say crows I do not mean rooks, which in looks are very
similar to crows but in habit entirely different.

If you see one rook, you see many. They are very gregarious

and can easily be distinguished – at least at close range – by the fact that they have a dirty grey growth round the base of the bill.

A crow's beak, no matter whether he be the hooded variety or carrion, is shiny black all the way from base to tip.

I've seen no hooded crows in these parts, but elsewhere I once saw a hoody attack a very weak thrush at a bird-table, knock it off and fly away with it.

Before we went to bed last night snow had started to fall, and was beginning to lie on the ground. The outside temperature registered eight degrees of frost.

When I arose in the morning, there was snow all over the place. I went out, after getting the fire going, to find ten degrees of frost and both water-butts iced up; daytime, but barely a light and not a bird to be seen or heard.

By the time I had sprinkled the birds' cornflake ration along the wall and returned to the house, Ann was down and making the tea. We looked out, bird-counting along her wall. Simultaneously we exclaimed: 'The big blackbird isn't there!'

Out we went to where that bird usually roosts and, the third bush along, there he was. Huddled up close to the trunk, eyes closed, feathers fluffed out. And he was stiff. My wife held him in one hand while loosening his claws with the other and we took him into the house.

There the routine is standard – and this is the third time we have had to use it this year. First it was a frog, next a thrush and now a blackbird. The frog needed no food; the thrush is now a member of our tribe and sensibly sleeps under a laurel bush in the garden, well sheltered. Soon the blackbird had recovered enough to attack cow cornflakes in a saucer, scattering them all over the place. Before he had finished we took him out to the stone wall and put him there, laying the contents of the plate before him.

By the time we returned to the house, he was being attacked by a blue tit but fortunately was now able to hold off his assailant. In view of the forecast, my wife put out another ladle of cow cornflakes and crushed barley.

Two hours later, the birds were still there, pecking away. And remember: in weather like this carbohydrates are essential to combat extreme cold. With a bird's quick digestion they are almost immediately assimilated.

A Hare Comes for Breakfast

Last night, a little before midnight, the barometer started plummeting and soon snow was falling, not from the west as had been forecast, but from the bitter north. By the time I went to bed there was a thin powdering on the ground.

This morning I got up earlier than usual, for the night's snow had made the day get lighter half an hour earlier. On going downstairs I was amazed to see that the barometer had dropped four-fifths of an inch since midnight.

There were several inches of snow on the forecourt and the outside temperature was two degrees below freezing. Not much, you may say, but added to an icy wind from the north, bitter is the word.

I pulled back the curtains preparatory to letting the cats out for a walk before Ann comes down (after her mug of tea) and sets out the bird food. Before doing that however she gets the cats back and they stay in the house until dusk falls and the birds have gone to bed. Just as I was about to open the window, what should I see but a hare unconcernedly loping across the forecourt, not three yards from the window, evidently having come in through the drive gate.

I watched it as it passed and when just beyond the front door it turned sharply left, the other side of the wheelbarrow-load of logs (now all heavily covered with snow) and disappeared.

I knew exactly where it was going and decided not to let the cats out until it departed. It had gone into the nearest loose box for its breakfast. Hares and horses (not to mention donkeys) take but little notice of each other, except that horses are very careful never to tread on a hare.

There is an exception to this rule, however. Once I saw a mad March hare attack a full-grown Shire stallion weighing over a ton. The attack was made frontally with confident but restrained power, very menacing. The great horse looked down and snorted and the hare stopped dead about three feet from its nose, sat up and adopted the first position of an old-fashioned boxer. I have been similarly attacked in the past – and that stallion evidently knew as much as I about such goings-on. He gave another snort of simulated fear, turned on his heels and galloped away, raising both heels in a lethal kick when about ten yards from the hare. He galloped up to the gate to tell me about it but I already knew. These attacks are perfectly harmless and only made to impress the doe, who is quietly sitting some distance away watching the incredible bravery of her swain. And we both agreed that this doe must have been enormously impressed.

The hare in the loose box would find plenty to eat under the manger; hayseeds in abundance, not to mention at least a couple of handfuls of flaked maize and oats, all very nourishing. Sure enough, it took a good twenty minutes to make its meal, during which time there was not a sound from Patchy and Rebecca, both in the same loose box.

Then the hare came out and as it did so a little sun shone gently and flooded the forecourt, although the snow clouds to the north were still black and menacing. It sat up in the sunlight and proceeded to wash its face (all rodents are very particular about this after a meal).

Then it got down on all fours and departed whence it had come, with a comfortably full belly that would last it for twenty-four hours at least. I let the cats out, then took a mug of tea up to Ann.

An Odd New Resident

Years ago I wrote about a small polecat that I had rescued from an old-style (and now illegal) gin trap. Although I had been accustomed to handling ferrets – both white and fitchett – from childhood without ever getting bitten, this little jill bit me on a finger as I was releasing her from the trap before taking her home, and I found myself with a very nasty case of blood poisoning.

When I wrote about this I had several letters from readers, more or less evenly divided. Some said that I was talking through my hat; that the real polecat (*Mustela Putorius Anglius*) had been extinct in Great Britain for over a hundred years. They were wrong. In the last fifty years the polecat has been slowly returning until now they are quite common in various wilder parts of the Welsh hills.

The other group of writers told me that polecats were common, several of them saying that they possessed 'polecat or fitchett' ferrets.

The latter certainly are or were quite common before the advent of myxomatosis which killed off the rabbit population and put an end to ferreting for rabbits. The fitchett ferret was *not* pure polecat, only a cross (sometimes very far removed) between the old polecat and the albino white ferret with red eyes.

Today, years later, the real wild polecat, locally known as 'foulmart' because of the appalling stink he is capable of producing when angry or frightened, is getting quite common up here, particularly now there are forestry plantations all over the place.

The other day, while putting the horses out after a warm night in their loose boxes, I noticed a small hole about three inches in diameter in a bank in the house-paddock not twenty yards from our front door.

I wouldn't have seen it had it not been for a piece of bright blue plastic torn out of a bag of fertilizer, part of which had been macerated by sharp teeth. Bits were still lying round the entrance and a trail of them dwindled down the entry until they could be seen no more.

Something lived down that hole and I wanted to identify it. It could have been a field-mouse, a small grey squirrel, a stoat or a weasel. There were small claw-marks in the entry, but I couldn't identify them.

Last Thursday we had a heavy snowfall and I inspected the hole. There were well-defined footmarks both coming and going, which either belonged to a very large stoat or a rather small polecat; so I decided to watch.

All hill farmers always have a gun handy because if they did not they would go bankrupt in two or three years. There are in these hills many predators, such as carrion crows, magpies, ravens and foxes. If these were allowed to increase without being kept down, in five years there would be more foxes than sheep in the hills. The wild bird population would decrease to the point that they would no longer be able to control the many creepy-crawlies that destroy crops. But in this case I needed no gun, for the ferret family (weasels, stoats, polecats, and pine martens) serve a very useful purpose. Their main diet consists of mice and rats. They have become the guardians of our stack-yards and no hill farmer in his senses would ever take a gun to one of them.

Rats and mice living in the haystacks eat the grain that feeds the stock. Stoats, weasels and polecats roaming the stackyards are therefore money in the farmer's pocket – bar one small point and this is it: one must put chicken netting not only all round the fence of your hen-run but on top as well, so that the poultry is protected on all sides.

Yesterday evening I had my reward. The sun was just going down and there was promise of a very cold night. Out of that small hole there poked a little black muzzle. By degrees emerged a small, apparently black body, slinkily and snakily, followed by a bushy black tail.

She (it looked like a jill) sat up on her hind legs, forepaws dangling in front, head turning this way and that, sniffing the air. I didn't move. And presently off she went, a gracefully un-dulating little body, down the hill and away.

February

Our Animals Go Skating

I looked out recently an old weather-book published in 1830. I've been remarking for years with increasing emphasis how the weather has changed since I was a small boy. I remembered something from that old book which I hadn't thought of for years – and there it was, sure enough, with a lovely engraving of a snowed-up mail coach:

There can be as much hard weather in February as in any month of the year. Snow has been known to lie so thick on the roads that mail coaches have been stopped for days on their journeys. ...

Yet we have been calling February 'Fill-Dyke' for more than a hundred years and, with few exceptions, Fill-Dyke has suited its character. I hope we don't get too much snow this time.

The bedroom and living-room windows were spattered with what appeared to be recent rain when I got up this morning. I went outside to look and nearly took a purler. The whole surface of the forecourt was covered with very small globules of clear ice – and that is what the spatters on the window were: ice, not hail, that had stuck to the relatively warmer windows.

Later, my wife and I went out to gauge road conditions, and it was like skating in ribbed rubber soles.

On letting Gretchen and Meg out for their usual run, they bounced down off the front door step with their usual careless abandon at maximum speed and turned right to go through the gateway of the drystone wall. On the turn they both fell sideways and slid for a couple of yards. They did not stay outside for longer than necessary but returned at a sober gait to the house, looking more subdued than I have ever seen them.

When Patchy came out of his loose box after breakfast he too stepped forth boldly on to the forecourt and slid – fortunately forward and without falling down. Having recovered and stopped dead, he collected his feet into the correct rectangle and turned his head and neck to look reproachfully at Rebecca, his devoted friend.

Rebecca got the idea immediately, because all donkeys know from babyhood that they are much more intelligent than horses. (And so do horses.) So, stepping very carefully, Rebecca walked past Patchy, negotiating the five yards to the gap like a cat on hot bricks, followed similarly by Patchy without further mishaps. Then they were on rough ground; not soft certainly because it was already frozen at least twelve inches down, but non-skid. Once there they trotted carefully a few yards further down and started to graze on the short grass that the blizzard had laid bare.

This shows how stupid human beings can be. I had had the example of two dogs and two equines behaving as they should not behave on a skating-rink. And yet I went out to gather a few armfuls of logs for the fire. I forgot all about their terrifying experience.

I was just cursing the fact that another victim of the blizzard had been our metal wheelbarrow (it had been blown over and over from one end of the yard to the other), when suddenly I started to skate and though wildly waving my arms could not stop. Fortunately I kept the upright position until I was brought up short by the muck-heap, into which I fell headlong. It was frozen solid, so I didn't sink into it but only bumped my nose. After that I went very carefully.

One other thing happened that I have never seen before. That same afternoon we both saw a large cock blackbird helping himself from one of the coconut shells which my wife fills with fat. In no amateur manner he turned upside down like a gymnast, getting a beakful and then rising to a perpendicular position with the help of his wings. He must have eaten nearly an ounce before he had had enough and flew away to allow the tits to resume their feed.

A Badger Sits
down to Dine

In weather like this, with maximum temperatures of −2°C.
by day and −20°C. by night, one takes calculated risks, particularly if one has a Land Rover with its epicyclic low-ratio
four-wheel drive.

In the hills I'll always take a calculated risk, if it doesn't in-
volve anyone but Ann and myself. One has to, in exceptional
circumstances like this sudden Arctic spell, especially when de-
pendent animals are involved.

It means keeping on the go all the daylight hours, carrying
hay to them, and water, which we have to carry from a long
distance. Our water supply and all toilet arrangements have
been frozen up for ten days. This is all Land Rover work, but
fortunately our garage knows the difficulties and keeps us
supplied. We are also having to carry our logs because our
normal supplier cannot get up here in his lorry.

This morning I came down early, just as dawn was breaking,
and, on peeping out through the living-room curtains, was surprised to see an enormous badger carefully walking along Ann's
drystone wall in front of the house and nosing out here and
there a grain of flaked maize which had been left by the birds.

Now this badger has, for the last two years, been an
occasional visitor to us, generally messing about in the stables,
garnering a few grains of corn or flake to help out the ration.
But I had never seen her quite so close and knew that she really
needed what she was looking for.

So I went out and immediately she jumped off the wall, running down about twenty yards before hiding herself in the
blackthorn hedge.

I went to the stables and got a dipper-scoop of barley and,
taking it out to the far end of what will one day be our kitchen
garden, I up-ended it on a nice dry hillock where no snow had
collected.

I then retired to the house, closing the door quietly, and took up a stance in the living-room a few yards back from the window so that I should not be seen.

Five minutes passed. Out, very cautiously, came the badger, not creeping but walking with all eyes looking in every direction. She walked up to the barley, sniffed it, walked all round it with nose down to see if it might be trapped and then sat down.

It was almost as though she were about to wrap a napkin around her neck but she hadn't got one. So she sat down with legs widely straddled on each side of the barley. Then she set to, not greedily but selectively, and in a very few minutes that barley – about three-quarters of a pound, absolutely stuffed with calories and carbohydrates – had disappeared.

Casually brushing off her nose and whiskers, she got up and shambled off down the hill where she lives, about a quarter of a mile away. And my little day was made.

My only worry was that recently it has been claimed that badgers are carriers of tuberculosis and in the lowlands of England are being exterminated for fear that they may infect cattle.

Up here in the hills I do not think this is possible. After a long life of observation I am convinced that hill animals do not suffer from tuberculosis.

A Cat called Cleo Comes to Stay

This winter has been harder than any since 1963, and that was said to be the worst since 1742. The wind, having started as a south-easterly gale, has now settled due east-by-south, which means that it is sweeping all the way from Russia, through Poland, into Germany, and now to us.

However, we were well stocked up with everything we might need; but there is always the unexpected to cope with.

Three nights ago we had a telephone message from people

then quite unknown to us. They had recently bought a small-holding near here, but it is right on a fairly busy country lane. They had a couple of good Siamese yearling she-cats; could we possibly take one or both, as fast as possible, please, because they didn't want them to be run over.

So off we set next morning, a calm day as yet but bitterly cold. We decided to cut a couple of miles off our journey by going straight over the top. The single-track road was hard and dry, until we actually came near the summit.

There before us spread a horrible sight: at a steep turn, the entire road was glassed over by spring ice for about two hundred yards, the outer side protected by heavy steel girders to prevent traffic dropping at least two hundred feet to a stony bottom.

I put the Land Rover into low-ratio four-wheel drive, got into first gear, and gingerly started up, trying not to look right where there was an unprotected sixty-foot sheer drop.

Half-way up we began skidding. So I slowed right down, then gently accelerated again. Thank heaven the new tyres bit and on we went, round the guarded corner, to see another two hundred yards of smooth ice before us.

However, we made it without disaster, deciding to come back by the valley road. It was the nastiest quarter-mile I have negotiated for many years.

We finally got to the cat-owners and, to cut a long story short, decided we could take one of the Siamese cats. Half an hour later, we returned along the valley road with our new member of the family, Cleo, quite happily reclining in my wife's arms, looking with great interest out of the window.

On getting home Cleo had to be introduced to the animals. The two dogs bounced forward barking a welcome, but Cleo silenced them with a loud, very clear warning such as they had never heard before. Since then, they treat her with great respect.

She could not make out our Persian cat, thinking it was a dilapidated bath mat. For a whole day she growled and spat at Puss, but I'm glad she went no further: while Puss looks huge she only weighs 5½ lbs, and although Cleo is short-coated and looks quite small by comparison, she turns the scale at 7 lbs.

Puss was rescued by Ann from some squatters who were living in a derelict house about two miles away. They had the five-week-old kitten hung up by its tail. Our vet said he might as well let her go as she would never survive, but with Ann's care Puss became a very beautiful cat. Of utterly unknown parentage, I believe she would win a prize in almost any cat show as she is a full smokey or blue Persian.

However, they are all now the best of friends, and we were really surprised at the way Cleo, having cased the joint, settled down from the start and has not shown the least inclination to search for her old home. Long and happily may she live here.

A Tired Bird Drops in for a Meal

Weather-wise it is dismal, with cold winds and stinging rain. But at this time of year we are prepared for it.

So are the horses, and their nurse, little Rebecca the donkey, wise far beyond her years and loving them dearly. They are all in their shared loose box.

Far down the paddock in one of the sheltered spots in this area of old stone walls lies a ewe with a new lamb; too early in the year – but this kind of thing does happen.

I took her a measure of oats and an armful of hay early on and found them dry and happy; they'll be all right because in front of the overhung hole in the stone wall that the ewe found there is a big bush with a tangle of bramble in it that will keep the wind away. She does not belong to us but no matter. There will be shelter there for her as long as she thinks fit. I do not know to whom she belongs because her brand (the tar-mark made on her wool last year after shearing) was obliterated. She is a native-bred Welsh Whiteface and, as such, capable of surviving the hardest winter conditions.

My next concern was to provide food for the small birds. We no longer use a bird-table because Patchy soon found out about its advantages. It was exactly the right height for him to scratch his backside on, and as he is a very hearty scratcher when the mood is on him, it didn't last very long.

Nowadays we generally scatter the bird food (except for suet and coconut hanging in a nearby tree) on the forecourt in front of the house. But today it was raining hard and would soon have been washed off. So I put it on the window-sill. Almost immediately the sill was full of birds: two robins, several chaffinches, house sparrows, our two wrens and numerous great and blue tits. I sat nice and warm inside and watched, fascinated.

Once there was a scattering as a pigeon alighted with a great fluttering of wings, and started to peck delicately and selectively. But they knew that this was no dangerous bird, and came back again.

Then the cats ruined it by quietly jumping up on the broad inner sill and crouched, tails gently waving, intent on the birds outside. I had not thought of this as they had both been fast asleep on the sofa, far from the window. So I shut them up in the kitchen until such time as the food should be finished, and went on watching.

Then I noticed a ring on one leg of the pigeon, denoting that it was a carrier, either lost or (more likely) suffering from travel-fatigue. This often happens and if ever we see a trusting pigeon strutting up and down on the roof, we know that it will be up there for two or three days and put out food accordingly.

It was a pleasant sight, soon to be destroyed by a brazen bray as Rebecca galloped at full speed from the stables, followed at a sedate canter by Patchy. And I knew what this meant: my wife had returned from her shopping. So I went out and there she was, coming down the drive.

Two Barn Owls Pay a Visit

Recently my wife and I found that we have been putting on weight and we decided that the only remedy was to do more walking.

One morning, after breakfast, we set out to climb a nearby

hill despite the fact that there had been a downpour which had lasted thirty-six hours.

I had very nearly left my spyglass at home, because this is the dead time of year when most wild life keeps under cover – particularly animals that are largely nocturnal. This applies to most birds except the predators such as the raven, carrion crow, magpie, and buzzard, as these birds are always on watch for carrion.

Badgers in any case are very seldom seen by day, and we shan't see any foxes in daylight unless we get deep snow and hard frosts. For the moment there are many small animals about by night and, since myxomatosis, foxes have learned to eat a lot of roots and some berries. But if frost makes roots impossible to get and snow slows up the getaway speed of rabbits and hares, foxes will be seen all over the place and farmers will have to guard their poultry.

Anyhow at the last moment I decided to take the spyglass and when we got to the top of the rough little mountain was glad I had because in the valley eight hundred feet below we could see a road covered with water and only visible by the hedges on both sides. A solitary horseman was riding along and I put the glass on him to see that the horse was nearly knee-deep. The whole of that part of the valley – over a quarter of a mile across – was flooded and in the middle a twisted line of furious water showed the main stream.

Over a little knoll four buzzards were circling high, coming lower all the time; I expect they had found a drowned sheep on the edge of the knoll and would feed well.

Then appeared a farmer on a tractor coming fast along the road and we both burst out laughing. For the tractor was fitted with a big scoop or spade in front, useful for shifting earth or snow. And in this scoop, a good six feet above the road, sat a well-muffled-up woman: Farmer Giles and his wife going shopping.

I remarked to Ann that although we hadn't seen much wild-life on such a horrible day, I bet that farmer's wife was as wild as could be stuck up there, sitting on an icy steel shovel all the way into town.

Puffing and blowing after the climb, we sat on wet heather and ate sodden sandwiches, followed by a warming drink of rum and blackcurrant from my flask.

Then we started home and, when inside our smallholding, saw the first really welcome sight of wildlife that day. On a very naked tree beside our cottage sat two beautiful barn owls that we hadn't seen before. As we approached they looked gravely at us but didn't move until we were right under the tree. Then they gracefully took off, lazily flying to another about thirty yards on.

I imagine they had nested last year in our barn, and we hope that they'll do it again this year.

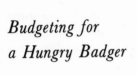 

Budgeting for a Hungry Badger

Up here it has been a pretty hard winter and now shows signs of getting harder. We have three hundredweight of breeze-blocks in the back of the Land Rover, two long-handled shovels, an axe and our ten-ton towing chain, so we can get through almost anything, besides being able (nearly always) to help others with less foresight to get out of their own troubles.

Yesterday we went down to the village to try to get some suet for our blue, marsh and great tits because that is about the only thing I know to keep life going in those lovely little birds in weather like this. I failed to get suet but instead I was allowed to cut bits of fat off various large pieces of beef in the butcher's deep freeze. The result was about three pounds of lovely fat at a cost of 6p per pound, which on arrival home Ann melted and used to fill four half coconut shells. These we hung up. They were immediately attacked by all our tits and that was that.

We had about a pound left over with all the necessary oddments that you'll always find if you render fat down. And that gave us another idea. In the snow on the forecourt that morning we had seen the footprints of our resident badger, seeking here and there for something to eat.

So Ann, melting up that remnant again, added to it the

remains of our last-night's dinner, a few bits of gristle, some
mashed potato, a few brussels sprouts with the rich white sauce
in which they had been cooked, left-over gravy and some salt.
When cooled and solidified into a rough ball weighing about
2 lbs, we put it inside the nearest loose box knowing that the
horses wouldn't dream of touching it. Horses are strict vege-
tarians. And there we left it.

Last night it snowed – albeit lightly – and there is more to
come. But this morning when I went out, there in the snow
were the footmarks of our questing badger. Obviously he had
had no further questing to do. He had gone straight into that
loose box. He had found that lump of highly-nourishing fat-
cum-protein. He (or she) had sampled it, tidily polishing up
the bits, and had decamped with the lot. Good luck to him or
her; at about 4½p per day, we can afford to keep him (or her)
alive.

*A Couple of
Red Squirrels
Join Us*

After an uncountable number of tropical downpours we were
giving up hope of getting outside until today dawned bright
and clear without a cloud in the sky, and a touch of sun to warm
things up before I had even got the morning tea.

After breakfast we took a walk round the little farm.

There are many little stone walls on the place, some of which
were obviously made many centuries ago, thick, solid, and all
green with thick moss. In many there are ferns and, in those
that have had soil drifted up against them, there is thick heather
that in summer will be a glorious sight.

Ann and I were discussing where to run a new fence, with
one point always in mind: never destroy a stone wall, because
it was built with a purpose. The farm lies on the eastern slope
of the mountain, facing from north-east to south-east – and that
is where the worst winds come from.

These walls were built with just that in mind, and indeed the farmhouse and buildings are surrounded with them, so that in the worst weather the owner can go outside his door and see all his stock sheltering without going more than fifty yards away from the house.

The farm is small and we soon decided where to run the new fence. We were on the way back to the house when suddenly Ann stopped, pointing to the house, and there on the drystone wall were two red squirrels busily tucking in to the food the birds had left.

For the past many years red squirrels have been something of a rarity in this part of the world. Some say the grey squirrels have killed them or driven them off. Others believe that the red squirrels were decimated by a mysterious disease. Whatever the cause, they are now rare all over the country and this is a grievous shame because, unlike the grey squirrel, they were never harmful on a serious scale. At worst, in a hard spring, red squirrels rob small birds' nests of eggs. On the other hand, they are very beautiful and in places like this seem to have no fear of human beings. Also (unlike the greys) they do not seem to take up residence in the attics of houses, which can be a real menace.

We walked slowly up to these little beauties and they did not appear to notice us until we were within a few yards. Then they sat up indignantly and started to chatter.

We quietly walked into the house and continued to observe them through the living-room window. They calmly went on with their meal until suddenly the sky clouded over and it began to rain, a nasty cold drizzle from the east.

Very gracefully, almost in slow motion, the beautiful little beasts calmly made their dainty way across the forecourt to what will be the goats' parlour and bedroom. This was once a pigsty, built of mellow, moss-encrusted brick.

All it now lacks is a roof, because I removed the remains of the corrugated iron top. It didn't blend with the surroundings, so we are going to roof it with red tiles.

They ran along the wall of the pigsty, made a flying jump off it, and ran down. Wanting to see if possible where they had their drey, we followed them, not even having time to put our macs on. No matter; we walked along behind them very quietly, and were rewarded by seeing them vanish into what

I had thought was an old magpie's nest. Now we know it is not and are happy.

As well as having a pair of barn owls on the place we also have a couple of red squirrels, and will look after them.

A Hedgehog Wakes up Early

A warm southerly wind was blowing despite high clouds coming from the north, but the glass was rising, which meant that we would probably have a cold night with frost. I was going to see how the electricity men were getting on with the installation.

It has taken them an age to get round to putting the posts up, but within a month we should have power in the house and stables. We were wishing for a change in the weather because for the last month it seems that it has been one perpetual February Fill-Dyke. I've never known it wetter, which prompted me to think of a verse in one of the psalms: 'though Man hath his desires, God has his designs.'

The field I was crossing is the highest on the farm and the driest. The electricity men were digging a post-hole a little further on. Suddenly I was astonished to see a corpulent hedgehog slowly coming towards me. Now, this is unprecedented at this time of year, for hedgehogs go into deep hibernation just before the onset of winter, and stay in that state until spring. In this they are completely conditioned and should not be disturbed. If you wake one up out of this deep coma, it is almost certain that the animal will die. I know this to be true because once as a child I had a pet hedgehog (one of many over the years) and woke it up on a warm day in winter, thinking it might like a drink of milk. It certainly drank the milk and seemed to enjoy it, after which I put it back into its winter bed. Two days later I went to repeat the process and found it dead.

Later I told a naturalist about this and he advised me never to wake a sleeping hedgehog. It completely upsets their internal combustion system, or, as we say nowadays, their metabolism. Incidentally, I never put out anything for these useful little animals but bread and milk and meaty household scraps.

Here then was this hedgehog slowly walking uphill towards me, and I stood quite still. Presently he passed between my legs and for a moment I was at a loss to know what to do, remembering that all the portents said that there would be a heavy frost that night.

This one had obviously been disturbed by the men putting up the poles and the chances were that his winter nest had been dug up by them. Now the need was to get him into some other place as fast as possible.

I looked around. There were plenty of gorse-bushes which will eventually come up when I re-seed that paddock, but over on the far side was a splendid blackberry thicket.

I couldn't make him a nest of dead leaves, of which there were plenty lying about, because they were all soaking wet. But the ground under that thicket seemed to be perfectly dry an arm's length in. I picked him up, shoved him in as far as I could and left him there, pushing in several handfuls of leaves to hide the hole I had made with my arm.

There he should be safe for the rest of his sleep. I very much hope so, for they are extremely useful to have in any garden or on any farm. And don't you believe that old tale that hedgehogs suck the milk from sleeping cows. You hear it everywhere but I've never seen it happen and nor has anybody else I've ever talked to about it. They do more to eliminate slugs and snails than any other beast I know.

Come spring I shall know if he survived by any displacement of the leaves with which I blocked him in.

A Happy Event for Puss and Cleo

Purple Passion seemed an adequate name for the little half-breed Persian kitten when she first arrived from what cannot have been a happy home.

At five weeks old she only weighed seven onces; she was miserably thin and although one should never take so young a cat away from its mother, we had no qualms in doing so to her. In another fortnight she would have been dead; indeed, our vet said we would never rear her.

She was curiously coloured, with short-haired, all-black head and legs up to knees and elbows; her body, as long-haired as any Persian, was a purple-grey. As to the passion part of the name, she immediately fell in love with my wife and me.

On Cleo's arrival, aged one year, she knew her name, something that few cats do. When Purple Passion became no longer purple, her name no longer applied. In the hope that she might learn to answer it, we re-named her Puss, and, believe it or not, she soon realized that she was Puss.

The two cats were quite inseparable and spent a lot of time exploring the neighbourhood.

In due course nature had her way ... so we had to keep them inside all the time. But one night we had a late visitor who accidentally let them both out, where they stayed until late next forenoon. They returned sleek, complacent and ravenously hungry. Soon we knew that the worst had happened.

They kept us on tenterhooks. Then one night we found Cleo having a kitten on the kitchen floor. Ann put them both into her basket, but she immediately hopped out and produced another, putting this one in herself after cleaning it up. And this she did with every kitten.

While all this had been going on we had not noticed what Puss was doing. We had fixed up a box for her in one of the living-rooms to keep them apart in case of jealousy. Before Cleo had produced her last, Puss must have started on hers. When we looked in, there she was purring and licking her three. Nor was there any jealousy. We shall keep the best in each litter and find homes later for the others.

The little newcomers were healthy, hungry and noisy. Just from curiosity my wife weighed them; one monster weighed seven ounces, exactly what Puss had weighed when five weeks old! And the lightest weighed six.

The other night we found Cleo in Puss's carton, giving the kittens a copious drink, while Puss was doing exactly the same in Cleo's box. There is obviously no point in trying to keep them apart, so we are going to decant the whole boiling into one large basket.

Three of the kittens which we are keeping are tortoiseshell she-kits, and one is a black tomlet with queer white markings. As each mother obviously believes that she produced all the kittens, it doesn't matter if the three tortoiseshells get mixed up.

In any case, I've always been told that Siamese cats never produce their own colour or beautiful blue eyes when crossed; they pass on nothing but their awful voices. If this is true, we shall know which pair belongs to Cleo.

The Taming of the Marsh Tits

We have known ever since we bought this small holding that there were marsh tits on a large patch of rather swampy ground with plenty of the kind of food that these fascinating little birds prefer. We have always regarded them as rather shy because if ever we got too close to their swamp they would fly away.

Never once, until a heavy snowstorm a few weeks ago, have they come up to our daily handout on the drystone wall. The first three or four days there were only two of these quite unmistakable little birds. Although in bird books they are listed as being the same size as a blue tit, they are somewhere between the blue and great tits, about four and a half inches from beak to tail.

Marsh tits are extremely catholic in their choice of diet. In the bird books, insects and small seeds are the only foods mentioned for them, but it was noticeable from first taking their places at the bird-table that they will eat a lot more besides: crushed oats (horse fodder passed through the mincer for bird use), flaked maize (horse and cow variety), our most popular commercial wild bird food, household scraps containing minced left-overs of mutton and beef, mashed potatoes and root vegetables. It was perfectly delightful to watch them.

Yesterday there were four marsh tits and today, eight. I believe that the entire population of the marsh below our east field is invading us.

Ann nearly always feeds them while I watch either through the living-room window or outside at a respectable distance. On one occasion the boldest of the bunch actually perched on her hand while she was carrying a split coconut across the fore-court to hang up in the blackthorn beside a large lump of suet.

But this morning was the funniest thing I've yet seen: Ann was taking out a lump of suet tied to a piece of binder-twine for hanging up when one of the marsh tits attacked it and took a bite. Then it flew up and landed on her head, using it as his chopping block.

Ann jumped, as he had missed his suet and pecked into her scalp! He immediately flew off into the blackthorn.

But why are these little birds so tame now, when they have never come up for winter feed before? Can it be that we have not yet seen the worst of the weather?

March

I Uncover a
Sleeping Adder

The day before yesterday Ann, after rounding up the horses for their breakfast, returned with a sizeable hunk of rotten timber which she handed to me. 'I got that out of the hole in the bottom of the fifth ash from the stable end, the big one that sprouts out of that wide stone wall. It is a much bigger hole than we thought.'

This meant the tree would have to come down, because we can expect quite heavy gales in a month or two. We regretted having to lose such an old tree but were glad on several counts that it had happened at that point.

At present there is a shortage of fire-logs. Many local people are turning to wood-burning due to the ever-rising price of coal. This tree, felled and cut up, will keep our spring fires going for a couple of months. The cutting up we can manage ourselves with the chain saw but the felling, I realized on examination, would have to be done by professionals with all the right tackle and all precautions taken. A couple of tons of tree, possibly more than that, with a huge hole in its bottom is a dangerous proposition.

Felling the ash would mean that the birds nesting in it would have to find a new home. We believe a woodpecker nests in a hole half-way up; and we know that two pairs of wood pigeons have nested for three years near the top. There's nothing nicer to wake up to in spring than the soft cooing of nesting pigeons with their little song of encouragement to cattle thieves – 'Take two coos, ye fool, take two coos!' – which my Scottish grandfather told me when I was a little boy.

We were raking out the bottom when suddenly my wife said: 'Whatever is that?' There, just visible in a mess of dry and powdered wood, I could see the back of a fat little adder, comfortably curled up and quite motionless. Obviously he was fast asleep.

Well, we both like adders, or any kind of native snake, for that matter; they do quite a lot of good and, as for the adder, his bite is not much worse than the sting of a hornet and he is not a malicious little snake. He never bites unless trodden on, though this can be fatal in the case of a small dog.

I went to get our broad long-handled yard shovel and we scooped him up with that plus a comfortable amount of the dry punk in which he was nesting. We both knew of another tree, beech this time, on a piece of nice dry land some fifty feet higher than anything on our land. And we walked him up to that tree on the shovel.

Scraping out a hollow we made a nice place for him, carefully sliding him off the shovel into his new house. All this time he never moved but was obviously alive. Then we got a shovelful or two of earth which we built into a sort of parapet in front of the hole, thinking it would face the rising sun and wake him up nicely when it got a bit hotter.

He would get over the top and find himself in a better situation, drier and warmer than in his old home. He'd be all right. There was one last thing to do to make him quite safe. I got a piece of oily, well-handled rag and stuffed it under his parapet, just showing.

This would keep any evil beast such as fox, badger or polecat, from molesting him. All wild predators fear anything that smells of man.

Three Hares in a Dust-up

We had certainly not been looking for any signs of spring after that horrible ultra-cold spell which took most people by surprise.

But the snowdrops are blooming in the old garden and the daffs are coming up, although there is no sign yet of any cheerful yellow blooms.

This morning, however, we noticed a March hare cavorting about on a large patch of grass below the drystone wall which has been two years in the making and isn't finished yet. There was a big congregation of birds on it when suddenly we saw this hare.

Hares are crazy things at most times of the year, but this one appeared to be at his most crazy. When he was joined by another hare the usual mock battle commenced; all wind and water, as my father used to say, like the barber's cat.

For several minutes the battle went on until, in the natural course of events, it arrived on the bird food patch. None of the birds took any notice, except to hop out of the way if some unusually clumsy gambol threatened to mow a few of them down. But presently everything seemed to calm down and the hares, under the wall, went out of sight.

We went up to our bedroom where a good view could be had – and there were those two hares calmly eating cow cornflakes, side by side, as cosy as could be; all thought of fighting for possession of the doe – which was presumably hiding coyly somewhere near – for the moment forgotten. Then, out from a tussock of coarse grass, she appeared, hippety-hoppety on her way to urge the swains on to greater efforts. But, arriving on the scene, she realized what was up and fell to like the others, busily munching away. For the moment at least the March hares' thoughts had lightly turned from love to something more substantial, and under the circumstances we did not blame them.

But someone else did. Since the cold weather started we have had several magpies eating there. Normally they never come near the place because I wage war on magpies and carrion crows. But one has to declare a truce in the depths of winter and I must say the magpies behave themselves when times are hard, and their table manners are generally impeccable.

But not now. Intelligent birds, they soon worked out that about sixteen pounds weight of large furry animals would, if allowed, seriously deplete the food supply. There were two of them, presumably mates, and suddenly they both set on the hares, stabbing viciously at their backs with their sharp-pointed beaks.

The doe in particular jumped high into the air and went galloping away down the paddock to the swampy bit where the marsh tits normally live, followed by the two bucks, likewise jumping about to avoid the beaks. It was interesting to note that the magpies were being followed by three marsh tits and one cock sparrow, each attempting to get in a peck or two.

The interlopers disappeared into the coarse grass down at the bottom. The birds returned to the table and all was quiet again. Later on my wife went out to put another half-scoop of flake down, to replenish what the hares had taken.

A Baby Hedgehog Finds a Home

At this time of year people always ask me about baby hedgehogs, because this is when all hedgehogs have either produced or are about to produce their broods. And, as is obvious, the mothers having to provide rich milk for anything between three and eight babies are continually ravenous and between feeding times (about every hour and a half) have to be continually on the prowl.

Normally there are sufficient snails, slugs, beetles and so on locally without the hedgehog having to go far in search of food. But occasionally hedgehogs have to venture further afield, and that is why, particularly on fast roads on the flat lowlands, hedgehog mortality is common. It is tragic, but you cannot blame the driver, who is often unable to swerve to avoid a hedgehog, which could be dangerous to other drivers.

To my knowledge a mother hedgehog never deliberately abandons her brood. In every case an abandoned family of babies is the result of a road accident, or death due to a hungry vixen also seeking food with which to nourish her young – both fox and hedgehog are mainly nocturnal.

At the moment we have a young hedgehog running around the house, perfectly friendly with the cats, dogs and our donkey, Rebecca.

The first meeting of the hedgehog and Rebecca, however, was not entirely friendly. Rebecca came forward. The little hedgehog immediately curled up into a ball and left it at that. Rebecca boldly advanced and lowered her nose to sniff at the intruder. Then she jumped back outraged and, seeing Patchy, Ann's perfectly inoffensive and very well-behaved hunter, launched out a double kick at him, poor beast. Patchy jumped aside and came to me for comfort while the hedgehog, nonchalantly uncurling himself, waddled up the front door steps and into the living-room.

We have had him for about three weeks and in another three he will have departed. But he will remember that we are his friends and, if in need in the future, all he has to do is to come to our front door and wait until someone comes out.

How do you care for a very young and mumless hedge-piglet? If his eyes are not yet open you have only a fifty per cent chance of rearing him. If his eyes are open you have a seventy-five per cent chance, and if he is managing to get about reasonably, he'll make it. Remember that at this early age he is a milk drinker. Make up your cow's milk in half pints. Go to your vet and get from him a small lamb-sized bottle of Ovigest or Protogest, whichever the vet suggests. This is a powerful reviver of moribund lambs, and every good shepherd has a supply. Add half this bottle to half a pint of cow's milk (tinned or fresh), add a dessertspoonful of brown sugar, heat to blood heat and feed him every hour and a half.

When he becomes really active, teach him how to hunt for snails and slugs, and by that time he will probably have heard the mating-call and will be off. But you will have made a friend for life. Whenever he is hard pushed for grub, he will come to you. He will love you. And he will keep your garden free from all the worst pests. Give thanks to him for that, and look after him.

I was downstairs by sun-up, opened the living-room door and was greeted by a warm red glow of sun beaming through the curtains.

After putting on the kettle I went to take a bearing on this bright new sun to find it had risen but little north of southeast. So we are making some progress at last towards spring.

I shut up the compass and was going back into the living-room when I heard a strange noise from Patchy's loose box, which is next to my workroom. That is one of the beauties of the old longhouse style of farmhouse. Any untoward noise from stables and shippon can be heard anywhere in the house, a priceless asset in case of sudden emergency.

Having put the compass away and made tea, I went out to see what might be amiss. Patchy and Rebecca were standing side by side looking down with sympathy at a large badger lying flat and panting as though exhausted.

It was very thin after its long winter sleep and I imagine had probably woken up the previous day, when the midday temperature was an unprecedented 10°C., and emerged from his den to see what there might be to replenish his flapping belly.

One hind foot had a bright ring of brass wire wound round it and the other end of the wire was trapped under a round stone which Ann had brought in a few days ago because she thought it might be a piece of prehistoric sculpture.

Indeed, she may be right, because two holes (for eyes) had been bored into it, under which was the top part of what may have been a nose. Below that there was a clean break; mouth and chin did not exist. However, it weighed quite a lot and was more than enough to anchor a badger weakened by the long sleep.

Leaving things as they were but shutting the door, I returned to the house, got Ann up, pocketed a pair of wire-cutters and looked for a sack. An old-fashioned jute sack would have been ideal, but alas, they have practically gone out of use. Nowadays, sacks are either made of paper or, more commonly, of plastic. So I had to make do with an old coat.

We went to the stable to find the badger still lying flat. Handing the wire-cutters to Ann, I dropped the folded coat over the head and fore-part of the body, falling to my knees to grip the coat both sides, with my hands on the middle to hold the animal down. But it hardly struggled at all.

My wife, on her knees, was working one cutter under the wire and that was no easy task – but finally the wire snapped.

It was an ordinary wire rabbit-snare which was responsible. The badger had obviously walked straight into it and, on realizing that it was caught, had struggled on, pulling the long peg out of the ground and getting away with the whole lot. Then, coming to us for food, had jammed the wire under the stone.

We got up and stood back, the badger still lying down. Ann fetched a dish of water and a piece of meat and we left them there, horse, donkey and badger, shutting the door on them.

Half and hour later we returned. The meat had been eaten, the water drunk, and the others were still munching their hay. We opened the door. The badger, that had backed into a corner, ran out and limped away down the hill.

Hares on our Vegetable Patch

It was not the sort of day you would expect to see the nuptial battle between two March hares for the favours of a doe. Nor would one have expected to see it taking place on a square patch the other side of the concrete forecourt, not ten yards from the house.

My wife and I were watching from the living-room window, but were not the only spectators. Three cats were watching this dance-cum-battle, sitting in a row on top of the woodpile lying against the house in front of the living-room window.

There was nothing to be feared by the fighters as our cats have a wholesome respect for hares. One kick from the hind feet of a full-grown buck will send a smallish cat – such as all ours are – flying several feet through the air, temporarily winding it. In any case, these March antics make a randy buck doubly aggressive. I have seen one attack a large cart-horse – much to that animal's interested amazement – while I have been attacked more than once.

There was another spectator in the form of Meg, who was standing up between us with her front paws on a chair, perfectly fascinated, growling low in her throat with her hackles up. Never before had she seen not just one hare but two so tantalizingly close.

Gretchen was lying asleep, or pretending to, on her rug in front of the fire, taking no notice. Many times in the past rabbit and hare have made a fool of her. A very fast runner, she never learned to make a right-angle turn at full speed until, probably having watched a fox performing the manœuvre, she made her turns by jumping straight up into the air and twisting before coming down. Even that was not good enough, for by the time Gretchen had made her turn a three-legged hare would have gained at least ten yards.

As far as we know, Meg has never chased a hare and now she was quivering with eagerness to be up and at 'em. In any case, Meg would make no better showing than Gretchen, as already she weighs quite a bit more than the latter and in another year will probably top the eight-stone mark.

The reason we were able to watch this battle unnoticed was almost certainly the dense fog cutting visibility to less than twenty yards. All was shrouded in mysterious grey, adding romance to this nuptial battle scene.

We could not see the doe, who was certainly watching, probably on top of the overgrown wall, which in itself is a natural rock garden, topped by a long row of blackthorn. However, the battle soon came to an end.

The smaller buck landed a terrific kick on his adversary, throwing him right into the dip at the bottom of the garden. The winner immediately dashed to the wall, jumped over it and disappeared, presumably with the lady of his winning.

There was no sign of the vanquished, so we went out with Meg to investigate.

There he lay looking most uncomfortable and waving his front paws. Meg growled but Ann told her to shut up. I slid down into the dip and he made no attempt to get away, just looked at me with eyes that might have been frightened or not; I couldn't tell.

I picked him up by his fore-part and his hind legs dangled limp. He might have a dislocated spine but I thought not; his ears were worn and torn and he generally gave the impression of an old roué long past his best.

Probably this would not turn out to be his last fight, if my spot-diagnosis turned out to be right: a sharp attack of lumbago. You know how agonizing that can be if it comes on suddenly when digging a row in the garden.

We took him inside, keeping a careful eye on Meg. Puss, in my rocking chair beside the fire, opened one eye and shut it again. Gretchen, lying on her foam mat, did likewise. Only Meg, hackles flat and not attempting to bark or growl, sniffed the supine form with interest as I laid it down on her foam mat.

In the case of animals it is always best to give them the rest cure, which is their own remedy. Once we had a cat whose back was either broken or dislocated by a fox. He lay in the living-room for three weeks eating nothing but a little milk from time to time. Then he got better.

Now this hare just lay resting. On the second day he was hobbling around quite happily. He ate some salad my wife gave him with evident enjoyment and on the third we put him on the doorstep, leaving the door open so that he could return if he felt like doing so.

Slowly he hopped across the forecourt but not to the garden that had been the scene of his defeat. He turned right and departed up the drive.

Meg watched him go and then looked at us with sad eyes. We had deprived her of a new playmate.

Mother Rabbit Defends her Baby

I was looking out of the living-room window, when I saw a skirmish on the little hill to the south-east and about sixty yards away. Feathers were flying.

A big doe rabbit was fighting a kite, and I could see clearly that it was a kite, not only because it was bigger than a buzzard, for which it can be mistaken, but because of its forked tail; the kite is the only one of its congeners to have a swallow-like tail and it cannot be mistaken. The rabbit was attacking the kite at full speed, doing its best to drive the huge bird away; the kite was trying to get at a very small baby rabbit lying stretched out about two feet higher up the hill. I rushed outside and yelled; it bounced high in a vertical take-off and was immediately airborne, reaching full speed in six feet or less. It flew off fast in a northerly direction, back to the Tregaron district, whence it had obviously come. From one claw there was suspended a tuft of rabbit hair, which fell off and drifted down to the ground. There are, so they say, four or five pairs of kites permanently up there, the pride of local and visiting ornithologists.

I stood in the doorway thinking how stupid rabbits are, mating almost all the year round. That infant must have been at least three weeks old, born in the latest cold snap, quite the worst time of year to make an appearance. But by now it was sitting up, its mother poking her nose into it here and there as though determining the damage. Apparently there was none. One more impatient push in the behind elevated that little bunny on to its legs, and the two of them vanished into the scrub.

We appear to have only four members of the hawk family up here, the commonest of which is the buzzard, a large and beautiful bird. Twenty-odd years ago he fed mainly on young rabbits and carrion in winter. When the rabbits went, after myxomatosis, the buzzard, like many another wild thing, had to change his eating habits. It was so difficult that it seems they did not breed from 1955 to 1957.

Now they are making a comeback, and are quite common: useful to the sheep farmer too. If there is a very sick or dying sheep, it can be spotted from many miles away by the buzzards circling high overhead, waiting for it to die.

Next, in order of quantity, comes the little kestrel, a beautiful killer whose most noticeable characteristic is the strange ability to hover, apparently motionless and completely stationary, over the same spot for minutes on end.

Then, rather more scarce, come the sparrow-hawk and, most rare of all, the kite.

One day Ann was looking through the open mountain towards the lovely mountain range, which is our view from northeast to south-east, while I was dozing in the rocking-chair.

Suddenly she jumped up, went to my workroom and returned with my spyglass. She focused on something outside and turned to me, telling me to come and see. I went over and there, within forty-five yards of the open window (with two cats lying on the stone sill outside), was a female kestrel.

The kestrel was sitting in a most obvious position on the top twig of a dead spruce. She was in easy gunshot-range from the window; she could see the cats; she could see us and watch our every move. Yet there she stood on that twig, throwing us a glance from time to time. Her gaze was mainly directed at something underneath her. We watched that beautiful little hawk for perhaps half an hour and then, just to test her, I went out of the front door, round to my workroom window to see the outside thermometer. She never moved.

Later Ann walked slowly down to her and only when my wife was within ten yards of that tree did the kestrel fly away with strong, slow wingbeats down-valley.

One thing was certain: she had not been in that tree, as we had suspected, with a shotgun pellet in her body.

We got over the fence and saw what she had been watching. A male kestrel was stuck under a piece of old barbed wire. Ann hopped down and got him out, taking good care not to get bitten and we returned to the house.

In his case a shotgun had been the cause. Just one pellet had glanced off the outside of the outer wing-bone, almost cutting through one of the strong primaries just above the skin. This, though not crippling, must have been very painful with every small movement. But it was easily fixed. I pulled out the whole feather, root and all, with a pair of thin long-nosed pliers during which operation the kestrel gave me a sharp peck. After that, a squirt from the antiseptic aerosol which we always have handy in case of such minor surface injuries to man or beast, was all that was necessary.

We went out again after I had put some of the blue stuff on my bite. Ann had the kestrel in her hands.

By the way, in this species the sexes are very easily identified. The hen is brown, striated and with bars across her brown tail. The male has a blue or slate-grey head and tail, the latter not barred but with a much darker tip.

Ann opened her hands and for a moment he remained there. Then he stood up, pushing up and off, straight down the valley to where we had last seen the hen, and vanished. I expect they have a nest there in a tree. I hope they raise their young without any more attention from a shotgun.

April

Our Dogs Chase
those Crows

At the end of last year and into the new year, we had several fairly hard frosts – down to about –11°C. – but thank goodness our plumbing is modern. The expensive copper pipes didn't burst; only the washers at the joints went.

My wife wanted to have them repaired but I pointed out that we were still in danger of deep frost until the last week in April and might as well go waterless for three of four months to avoid the expense of two or three big plumbers' bills. After all, we can always go down to the village and get it at the communal pump, at the same time having a rewarding drink in front of a roaring fire at the local, which is beside the pump.

Towards the end of last month things started to go wrong. The wind dropped after we had been warned of a south-westerly gale. The mountains were covered with what is normally called a heat-haze. To anyone accustomed to the country something was about to happen. I, in our local (we had gone down to do the week's shopping and to fill up with paraffin), was laughed down, having forecast bitter weather and possibly snow.

This morning after breakfast my wife went down to the well, and its currently useless little motor-pump, to bring up half a can of water in each hand.

Then suddenly back she came, telling me to get the gun because carrion crows were eating all her precious frogs' spawn in the first-flow well.

I pointed out to her that the mere fact of her arrival and rushing back would have frightened them off – even had she been dumb – so that a gun would be useless. Instead, I pointed a few long sticks, got the sledge-hammer and accompanied her back.

Those crows had not been quite as intelligent as usual. As we went into the well paddock there they were, at it again, pecking away so busily that they didn't notice us.

'Fetch,' I whispered to the dogs, and away they went, getting within three yards of the black devils before the latter were aware of them. With a harsh croak each took off towards the east, and with mad barks the dogs took after them. The race was on.

Having to turn sharp right, Meg, the younger and less knowledgeable, went over like Charlie Chaplin on one leg, but without a cane to balance her. Gretchen, trained by running after hares, was more intelligent, stood up like a fox to turn and raced after them, so fast that she overtook them. Before they could gain height she had leapt at the last in line and came down with a tail-feather in her mouth. She trotted proudly back to me followed by a shame-faced Meg, one side all coated with mud. And, as a good retriever should, she gave me her feather which I put in my hat. The dogs' day had been made. We got down to work.

The frog-spawn seemed to be quite all right but, as I had suspected, one of the horses had nosed aside the heavy wooden cover of the well. Two long stakes on each side and in front of the cover, well hammered in, took care of that, and thenceforth the froglets, as soon as they developed, would be free to wander forth on the face of the earth, as long as they don't venture too far from us.

We Find our First Slow-worm

There is an old rhyme that used to be popular among all farmers, both in the lowlands and in the hills. It went as follows:

> Do your work well in all its stages,
> And you shall live well and have good wages.

So it was in those days. Up two hours or more before dawn to feed, groom and harness the horses, and up two hours after sunset to do that same work in reverse. An average of at least eighteen hours a day in summer, fifteen or so in winter, all the year round. In the hills it was somewhat harder but hill farmers employed as little labour as possible. They used their children as soon as they grew old enough to milk the cows and, later, to tend the horses.

I thought about this when we ran out of wood. The nights are still very cold up here. It was the weekend and no chance of getting Danny the Wood up until Monday or Tuesday. So down we went to the bottom of the paddock to saw up a spruce trunk, about ten inches thick at the base, about twenty feet long and weighing, at a guess, five or six hundredweight.

Having arrived there, we first needed to lever it aside with two crowbars, because all sorts of useful beasts lie under such protection, and one wouldn't want to hurt them. In this case it was just a question of a couple of quick heaves on the bars and it rolled aside. Immediately four fat frogs jumped out, possibly some of those which, a few days previously, had laid their spawn in a nearby stream.

My wife found it full of spawn about a week ago, for which we were glad, as frogs are more than useful to gardener and farmer. We didn't notice where the frogs went, probably into the stream running along the wall.

We moved up to the thick end of the trunk, and there was the first slow-worm or deaf adder that we have seen up here. No, the slow-worm is neither a worm nor a serpent, although at a casual glance the average person would undoubtedly class it as a snake, probably non-poisonous on account of its small head. Non-poisonous it certainly is. It has eyelids like a lizard, a bone-connection in front to both sides of the jaw and a notched rather than a forked tongue. All these are lizard characteristics.

In fact, the slow-worm *is* a lizard. But millions of years ago it decided that it didn't need legs like other lizards and let them wither into useless appendages. Little by little its scaly skin grew over them so that nowadays it looks like a snake. But is still has those useless legs under its hide. Unlike a snake, if you grab it by the tail it will leave that part of it in your hand and scuttle away to safety. In due course it will grow another one, not so well finished as the original and always showing the join.

The slow-worm we discovered slithered rapidly away, into the stream and out the other side, to lose itself in a crevice between two large stones. And there, of course, we left it.

These little reptiles are every bit as much use to the gardener as the frogs although their mouths are much smaller. They seem to specialize in the smaller whitish slugs as well as flies and the smaller creepy-crawlies.

Ten minutes later we were busy sawing up and splitting that day's supply of logs. We felt we had 'done our work well in all its stages'.

*Tartan Pounces
on her Mum*

For the first time in many years we have only four cats on the farm, two of which are dedicated hunters, mainly of mice and young rats. The other two are Cleo, a pedigree Siamese of great beauty whose arrival I have already described, loyally backed by her son Thomas the tom, a very pleasant youngster with the largest feet and the greatest number of fingers I have ever seen on any cat.

Tom was an accident, but a very welcome one. His papa was a neighbouring farmer's tom-cat sired some years ago by one of our own black polydactyls, or many-fingered cats. I brought the strain into this part of the country about eighteen years ago and they have slowly spread over roughly a hundred square miles centred on our old farm. For these little black toms are great travellers in springtime and become terrific hunters. Although half-Siamese, Tom takes after his wild forebears and is a short-coated black, small, with large ears and a perpetual purr. Tartan is Puss's daughter, so called for her Persian-tortoiseshell colour.

This morning as usual they ran out as soon as the window was opened, jumped into five inches of crisp snow, eight degrees of frost and brilliant sunshine. I went into the kitchen to get the morning tea started when I happened to look out of the window.

There on the sill stood a robin. We have two robins, a posh one who frequents the front side of the house and feeds on the drystone wall whenever it is replenished, and a peasant robin who uses the back side of the house and is there on the little granary window-sill every morning when Ann goes to feed birds and horses. His ration goes on that sill.

Now, here he was, tapping the window to attract my attention, strutting up and down looking very important and quite wide awake. I mention that because about five feet away was the menacing figure of Puss, crouched low in the snow.

Three feet to Puss's rear lurked another sinister shape: Tartan, likewise crouched, her tail waving as a cat's tail waves when about to pounce. All this time the robin was quite aware of what was to come, a pounce for which he was ready.

And the pounce came – but not as we had expected. Tartan suddenly launched her fluffy bulk, not at the robin but at her mother. Snarling and spitting, lashing out furiously with all paws, Puss rolled over and over down into the ditch that drains the house. The robin and I were nearly helpless with laughter, he to depart to the granary window-sill, I to make the morning tea. I have never seen a more disgusted cat than Puss.

But I forgot to mention Cleo. She *never* goes out if there is more than one degree of frost. Instead, she makes a beeline for the left side of the old cooking range. There it is nice and warm.

A Beleaguered Bird

Finally spring has arrived. Yesterday as we returned from the village, my wife excitedly drew my attention and said: 'Look, the daffs are almost out!'

Sure enough, every daffodil stalk had a torpedo-shaped flower-bud looking towards the sun and soaking up everything possible both of that and the warm, south-easterly breeze that made them sway gracefully.

The pussy willow had been out for quite a long time but today the tiny leaf-buds are much in evidence. Best of all, for me, the black-barked blackthorn trees in front of the house will be a blaze of white blossom in a few days if we get warm sun. From the window they are still black and gaunt except where there is lichen on the trunks, but if you go close to them, at the point of every brown flower-bud there is a minuscule point of dazzling white.

Then I went to see the daffodils in the garden, to which absolutely nothing has been done for about thirty years. In summer it is a wild tangle, practically impenetrable, but now the daffodils are having a lovely time.

Since quite late yesterday afternoon, all their buds have become full-sized blooms. Quite an astonishing but more than welcome sight.

My wife says that they are nearly a month earlier than last year. Up here, nearly eleven hundred feet above sea level, we are always at least a month behind the seasons as they occur in the Teifi valley eight hundred feet below us.

The blackthorn too is earlier than last year and I wonder what that portends? Last year we had an early spring and a drought in summer. I suppose that it could mean that we shall have a wet summer.

Later I went out for another look at the daffs and soon saw something much more interesting: two blue tits were building their nest in a hole in the wall, inside the garden. The hole was too small for any nasty predator to get in, bar possibly a weasel. But for two years now I haven't seen any kind of predator come anywhere near the cottage.

For perhaps ten minutes I watched them, until suddenly there were three tits building that nest, and I wondered whether they were a hippy colony. But I didn't wonder for long.

Suddenly one tit flashed in with a feather skilfully beaked. There was a furious squeak from inside the fortress and an answering squeak from the one with the feather; then came another, and the attack was on!

Obviously the tit with the feather was the intruder – an intruder now in a bad way, with one enemy in front, another behind (both attacking furiously) and himself in the middle of a small hole and quite unable to turn round. In such a horrible position he (or she) could not be expected to last long. And as far as we are concerned, we cannot have too many tits.

I was immediately attacked by the outside bird. I took hold of the intruder's tail and pulled. It came off in my hand so, drawing my trusty Biro, I inserted it 'twixt prisoner and wall, hooked it slightly inwards, and pulled gently.

Out came the inside tit, to be more furiously attacked than ever by the outsider. Both fell to the ground and re-engaged. I caught the tail-less intruder and carried it out to the forecourt blackthorn, releasing it. Away it flew, quite unharmed, but steering a bit erratically.

I don't expect it will try any more nest-robbing until its tail has grown out again. And serve it right.

We Spy on some Cheeky Voles

According to the calendar spring bursts forth on 21 March, but so far, at least up here, there are mighty few signs of any spring. It wouldn't surprise me at all if we don't get another snow-flurry or two in the next few days. As I write this a little after midnight, the outside temperature is down to –2°C. and it will drop further before morning. The wind has been between north-east and east for the last two days, which explains why it is freezing now and why, although calendar spring is now nearly three weeks old, no early-nesting birds have even begun to think about building their nests.

Ann's drystone wall along the front of the concrete forecourt is 24 inches thick and 33 inches high. The top is of earth, six to eight inches deep, anchored on both sides by flat stones to keep the soil in. Eventually it will be a bed for creeping rock plants, but for the last two winters it has served nobly as a bird table. A few days ago I noticed, along the ten paces of that top, there were about a dozen neat little holes dug down into the earth under the stones at the sides.

Obviously the work of bank or field voles or perhaps long-tailed field-mice; something that had evidently discovered that all kinds of high-protein edibles were cast down twice a day – for the birds. These little creatures, whatever they were, did not see why the birds should scoff the lot. Neither had we, for that matter, and decided to watch the next forenoon. So Ann, having replenished the table, half-filled a couple of coconut shells (hanging from the blackthorns by the wall), one with nuts and the other with rendered fat, and we retired to the other side of the drive gatepost about twenty yards away, nicely concealed, and waited.

We didn't have long to wait. Almost immediately the first little quadruped shot out of a hole on to the middle of the breakfast-table, and set to. Before he had taken a mouthful there were five or six more and from there on it was impossible to count. We now saw that they were bank voles, and of course a drystone wall with a nice earth top was right up their alley.

What amazed us was the fact that they did not bother the birds that had gathered nor the birds them. There were three pairs of blackbirds, a couple of missel-thrushes, twelve or more greenfinches and a bullfinch or two, but there was plenty for all, even with a couple of robins: and as everyone knows, robins are aggressive little beasts.

It was a really pretty sight because in the bright sunlight the little animals looked quite red, and at twenty yards with a powerful glass they appeared to be even redder; indeed, in some parts, they are called red voles.

Then, without warning, two magpies alighted on the wall. Simultaneously with the instant disappearance of every vole Ann jumped up waving her arms and yelling: 'Boo!'

Like something out of science fiction, those two birds vanished as if they had never been. The other birds had scarcely noticed their arrival. We resumed our positions but it was five minutes before a vole reappeared.

How a Tiny Leveret Fooled my Dogs

For thousands of years man has known about the protective colouring of certain animals, birds and fish, but seldom, if ever, made use of it.

I have often wondered why it was never developed in war, hundred of years ago, when soldiers wore red coats that showed up for many miles. The idea was evidently to strike fear into the enemy with brilliantly-coloured clothing and brightly-gleaming weapons and accoutrements. But finally, we imitated the animals, and benefited greatly therefrom.

The variations in behaviour from one creature to another is extraordinary and sometimes psychological. For instance certain birds, when danger seems to threaten, will hide their young chicks that cannot yet fly under a clump of heather or gorse. These chicks know what to do: they squat and freeze until the danger is over, be it a man with a gun, a prowling sheepdog or a fox. The mother bird will draw attention to herself, sometimes giving a squawk, hopping along with a dragging wing as though she has been hurt, clumsily trying to fly, limping along always in front of the danger until she has drawn it to a safe distance from her chicks. Then she flies straight back to where they are hidden, keeping a bright lookout until the danger is gone.

Only then does she cluck quietly to them and out they come, always in a tight little bunch, pecking about in safety near mum, learning to eat, learning to run, and eventually learning to fly.

Sometimes I wonder why the kingfisher is so brightly coloured and always come to the same conclusion, as anyone would who sees one flashing along just over the water, with or without a silvery minnow in its beak. Then, apparently without slackening its speed, it turns and vanishes into its hole in the river bank. The bright little kingfisher is the fastest thing on the river, and therein lies its safety.

I was given an interesting demonstration of camouflage yesterday morning. Earlier, I mentioned the mating battle (if you can call it that, because there is seldom much damage done) between two buck hares for the doe of their desire.

I was walking down the paddock with both dogs coming along just behind me, obediently to heel. Then, in a neat little form under a tuft of coarse grass, I saw a small leveret, crouching low, completely motionless and so perfectly blending with his background that I would not have noticed him had it not been for his bright eyes with their unwinking stare, gazing at me.

I turned slightly to one side, passing him within three or four feet, because I wanted to test something that I have often heard of but had never yet been able to prove.

The dogs were coming along as good as gold, a couple of feet behind me. Both of them have extremely good noses and will follow almost any scent, be it that of a rabbit, stoat, polecat, or adult hare. They'll chase them all except the polecat (who stinks) but never manage to catch them. Now they passed the leveret within three feet, and neither saw it nor smelled it.

It is said that although adult hares of both sexes have a strong scent, their young are completely odourless until they are grown enough to look after themselves. And this was apparently true. So we left the little beast in peace, and went home by a roundabout route.

Mystery of the Vanishing Birds

It was one of those days when, looking up to the sky, you wondered whether it would rain, hail or snow. And up here we are always scared of snow right through to the near-end of April. The sky was that nasty red rust colour all over and heavy rain had been forecast in our quarter.

It was cold. The humidity was very high. I was just saying to my wife, 'Thank goodness we don't have to go shopping today', when she pointed out of the living-room window.

'What on earth does that mean?' she asked.

I looked out.

There on the forecourt were fifteen chaffinches, messing about as if they were expecting their breakfast. Occasionally one of them made a peck at the ground, but they must have known that there wasn't much to eat on that bare concrete expanse.

It must be at least five weeks since we put out any food for the birds. They haven't needed it, as there has been the usual spring exodus of the creepy-crawlies that most of them live on, but there they were. I lit one of our pressure paraffin lamps because not only do they give a very good reading light, but they also provide heat, and we always use them rather than expensive electricity in cold weather.

Then it grew darker, much darker, and one by one those birds started to disappear. We went out to see why, and as we stood in the doorway those birds looked up at us. Two or three flew up and over the half-door of the nearest loose box, which is part of the house alongside my workroom.

In the loose box, Patchy and Rebecca were feeding alongside each other. There were three chaffinches perched along Rebecca's back and one on Patchy's chine. They took no notice of us, nor did the several others already pecking about on the floor. As we went out, the last two chaffinches flew past us into the stable.

Something was up. Those birds were all under cover. The glass had dropped two-tenths of an inch in half an hour. And that sky above ...

We went out, and in the next quarter of an hour had a two-day supply of logs inside the house, both shovels alongside the front door, four concrete blocks in the back of the Land Rover, ready for anything.

Outside there wasn't a bird of any sort to be seen except a pair of carrion crows hurrying silently homeward. The sky was heavier than ever.

Then, without further warning, down it came, an almost solid sheet of water out of a windless sky. Within half an hour at least an inch of rain must have fallen, and any small bird would have been dashed to the ground and quite possibly killed.

A raging torrent roared across the forecourt, half-way up the stone wall and over the dungheap, shooting at least half of it miles down the valley.

What I'd like to know is, how did those delightful and friendly little birds know it was time to get under cover?

Even I, weather-wise and with a very good aneroid barometer, didn't have an inkling, although I knew something was on the way. But those birds knew it would happen almost immediately. I can only guess that the insects, more weather-wise (with their delicate antennae) than the birds, had known first, and had all disappeared. The birds had taken it from there.

Gretchen Helps a Lucky Lamb

Our Easter lamb will not come to the table nicely roasted with all the trimmings. We will have just as nice a joint, just as well prepared, but it will be beef.

Our lamb will be prancing around the living-room as full of the joy of life as the poor little devil can absorb. And the way of it is this.

A few days ago I got up just as the day was dawning to brisk up the living-room fire and start things going. But first, having given the cats a drink of warm milk in the kitchen, I opened the curtains and living-room window to let them out for a gallop before Ann should come down and call them in for breakfast.

After the cats had galloped out I was just about to shut the window when I saw, on a bit of rising land which does not belong to us but marches with our south boundary, a small white blob which soon resolved itself into a lamb. It could not have been more than a week old.

As we had a lot of rain before the last light snowfall, that lamb had had a hard first week of its life, and now poor silly little thing had lost its mum – or so it appeared.

Calling Meg and Gretchen, our Rottweiler and Dobermann

guard dogs, I went out. Here I should say that both dogs, although very efficient guardians, have been brought up with one or two and sometimes more cade lambs being reared and fed in the kitchen. Gretchen in particular is extraordinary in this respect, because whenever we bring a motherless lamb in, she can provide milk within twelve hours of its arrival. She loves them.

Now we went out and when within a few yards of the lost little one, I made the noise of a ewe with a lost lamb. (All you have to do is to emit a single high note while waving your cupped hands in front of your mouth just like a professional mouth-organist.)

Immediately I did this Gretchen walked forward to the lamb and it trotted forward to her with exultant baa's. It nuzzled her underneath. She nuzzled it on the quarters, turned and came back, with the lamb bouncing along beside her.

Within two minutes we were all in the living-room in front of the fire. I dried off the little beast and laid it down between both dogs so that it could get warm. Then I went to the kitchen to look out the lamb bottle and teat, and warm some milk up for it. Ten minutes later it had fed, laid itself back between the dogs, and went to sleep.

That was early in the morning. During the day it had taken three four-ounce bottles of milk. Ann and I had been looking out for the ewe but could not find her.

Next morning we were more successful. She was tied up in a thick bramble-bush and one of her legs was badly sprained. We got her out, carried her down and put her into a pen. It is comfortable and, although the ewe seems to have lost her milk for the time being, we can take her lamb into the living-room and feed it milk until the ewe regains her own, which should be in a few days.

Meanwhile the lamb, which she gladly recognized, is feeding with us and in between feeds is with her mum, happy and comfortable in a draughtless small enclosure on deep, dry straw.

A Mouse gets
the Better of Puss

I was walking slowly down the hedge watching the burgeoning of spring as I went. It's coming, all right, if a bit late; the lateness can be accounted for by the very cold snap we had about six weeks ago.

The ash is rather behind but the sycamore is coming along nicely; elder, hazel and bramble are well on if not already in leaf.

I hope there will be a good crop of blackberries, rowan and elderberry this year because, with the present price of wines and spirits, one would be a fool not to make one's own wines and beer, and, if you take care, it always comes out well. We are going to experiment with swedes and turnips (we eat a lot of them as vegetables) this year, as potatoes will be too dear. We shall also try beetroot, mixing it with rowan berries which by themselves are very bitter. While thinking about all this and ambling along at about two miles an hour, I suddenly saw Puss the Persian and Thomas the tom (her son), plus Cleo the China Cat, all very intent on a tall hazel in the hedge.

In fact, Puss was half-way up it and could get no further because the branches or twigs were too whippy to bear her weight.

Not so her prey; a fat little dormouse was a good four feet higher up, and as much at home up there as any squirrel. It used to be said that the dormouse was related to the squirrel, but this is not so, nor is it in fact related to the numerous mouse family, but stands alone (at least in this country) in the family of *Muscardinidae*. It is called a mouse (even by naturalists) because it looks more like a mouse than anything else.

Dormice are extremely rare; indeed, in all the years I've been in these parts, this was only the second I had seen. Not only are they beautiful little beasts, but also appear to do no harm – at least up here where nearly every hedge is largely composed of hazel – because their favourite food is the hazel nut, of which they can make a huge store every autumn. They therefore do not raid vegetable and flower gardens.

This particular dormouse was as fat as butter – practically spherical – and did not seem at all put out. Indeed, once it seemed to cock a snoot at Puss, although it was probably just brushing a whisker and not intentionally taunting her.

But it annoyed Puss, who angrily waved her tail and snarled, crouching as though to spring, when the mouse knew perfectly well that she wouldn't dare.

But *he* sprang, exactly like a squirrel would on a slightly smaller scale, covering at least four feet and hitting a light branch on another tree a little lower than the first. He then climbed about a foot higher and prepared for the next feline threat, but it didn't come.

I started to walk away in the other direction. Puss protested as I held her in my arms, but she calmed down as I began fiddling with a knot of Persian fur in her neck, an operation she loves. Indeed, she will sit for hours in my wife's lap, eyes shut and blissfully purring, while the moulting process is gently urged along.

The other two cats dutifully followed close behind Puss and me. I think they realized that they would never catch that intrepid treemouse.

From time to time I looked back. As soon as the dormouse saw that we were off, he returned to his original tree, sat there for a minute or two, and then descended, to be seen no more. I expect his winter nest is far down some long-abandoned rabbit hole.

Meg Learns a Lesson

Some days ago all the hill farms (including ourselves), were crying havoc, as it had not rained for ten days. This can be dangerous in the hills. There is very little depth of soil in most places, with bedrock or loose shale beneath, and the topsoil is therefore very apt to get sunburnt, which kills off the grass-roots.

However, a few days ago there were some promising signs. The wind turned to the south-west and heavy storm clouds started to come up from the west. The barometer started to drop quite fast. All this meant that we would in all probability get torrential rain. In other words, the dry soil was going to get a welcome wetting.

By 3 pm the promise was fulfilled. It rained in an almost tropical manner for a couple of hours and, when it stopped, it seemed that in those short two hours the grass had grown greener.

We went out to enjoy the smell of fresh grass and have a look round. Were the springs running freely again? They were. Had the little well filled up again? It had. The rain clouds passed to the north-east and the sun shone bright.

Then we had another and fascinating demonstration of what warm rain will do. Generally speaking, slugs and snails are nocturnal and only come out around sundown to perform their deadly task of eating grass that should be otherwise employed. But occasionally, if you get heavy rain in daytime after a hot dry spell, they come out in force, even though the sun be bright, as it was now.

Great black bodies all over the place, guzzling away on grass that had had all the dust washed out, keeping themselves cool by the countless raindrops still falling off the grass.

We got a fascinating glimpse of how nature works. Like slugs and snails, hedgehogs are nocturnal beasts and the gardener's best friend – ninety per cent of their eating consists of garden and agricultural pests. But if there is a rain such as we had just had, they know immediately that there will be food for the eating without having to seek far for it, a bellyful in ten minutes or so, and then all the more time for refreshing sleep.

Up along the paddock lumbered a gigantic hedgehog, followed by four babies all in a single line behind, carefully stepping in mum's footsteps. We stood still and silent, watching.

Presently the mother stopped over a large black slug more than three inches long, and the babies all crowded round her. Obviously, overburdened with the many cares of motherhood, she was beginning to wean them, and they seemed to be enjoying the process.

But we had the dogs with us. Gretchen made no move, because once when she was a pup she had pricked her nose on a hedgehog. But Meg had never seen one before; here was something to play with, and with a glad yelp she bounded forward.

We said nothing. We knew what the result would be: before Meg got there those hedgehogs had turned into four little round balls and one great big one. Naturally Meg went for the big one, giving it a playful push with her nose. She sprang back with a yelp of utter consternation and ran to my wife.

By this time the hedgehog family had unrolled and scuttled off into the long grass, happily aware that they were invulnerable even to huge dogs. My wife and I walked back to the house, accompanied by a smug Gretchen and a rather shame-faced Meg. She won't try to fraternize with a hedgehog again.

The Jackdaws have Returned

At last the swallows are here, and this morning my wife went up into the loft over the stables to see just what was going on. I had seen one apparently making an inspection a week ago, but then he departed and we saw no more until two days ago.

This morning there were about four pairs present, flying high (when the glass is up, there is high pressure and the insects on which swallows feed fly high). At the same time two of them were obviously starting to build a new nest or repair an old one. My wife reported that two pairs were obviously on the build.

She also said that a pair of jackdaws were very busy excavating a hole up in the top of the eaves over the outside door of the loft where the bags of grain used to be hoisted in the days when it was used as a granary.

We were very glad to welcome them because it was the first

year they had come to us since we came here, and they are cheerful little birds. We had feared that they might chase the swallows away but of that there was no sign.

All was peaceful and calm; two lots of an entirely different kind of bird preparing to live in neutrality together.

At every place we have lived (either Wales or West Salop) there have been jackdaws nesting in or around the house. Only here did we miss them, and that was almost certainly because for long years this cottage lay derelict and unknown people had removed the granary floor for firewood along with its seventeen heavy oak beams which had been there since 1720. We cannot find it in our hearts to love people who would commit such a vandalism. And one cannot but admire such birds as agree with us.

We had watched those jackdaws cheerfully inspecting the property some weeks before and hoped they would decide in our favour. But we didn't imagine they would make such a job of it. Right up below the roof beam they are thoroughly excavating a nesting-place that will surely last them as long as the building stands, which should be (nuclear holocaust excepted) for at least two hundred years.

There we are: barn owls nesting in the upper part of my workroom chimney; swallows nesting where they nested last year; and jackdaws making a new nest in a building which has probably not known their presence since 1950.

Our only worry is that the swallows may have started too late in the year. It will be mid-June before the first clutch of youngsters hatch out; July before they learn to fly; the end of September at the earliest before they are fit for the long southward flight. I hope they don't raise a second brood this year.

The Jackdaw and the Cigars

> If the oak comes out before the ash,
> Then we'll only have a splash.
> But if the ash before the oak,
> Then we're sure to have a soak.

So goes the old saying which is sometimes true and sometimes not. It refers, of course, to the buds coming into leaf in the spring.

As to which tree comes first into leaf, I have an open mind. With the exception of the summer of 1976 when both appeared to bear at the same time (and we had a drought), for the last many years the ash has been in full leaf when the oak-leaves were only just bursting forth. But this year our five old ash trees burst forth only a few days ago and will not be in full leaf for many days yet, while the oak started bursting its buds long before the ash, and is now in full leaf. Are we in for an early drought, then? If it goes on it will play havoc with the harvest. I devoutly hope we get heavy rains within the next week.

The ash has for hundreds of years been reputed to have magic properties. If you had a small but sickly child, all you had to do was to pass it through the branches of an ash tree and it got better. There are countless tales of human beings and animals recovering from almost any sort of sickness, including non-mortal wounds, by touching an ash twig from a tree that had had a live shrewmouse buried in it. But in this age of unbelievers I have never seen it done.

However, there is a ray of more benevolent sunshine in the loft over the stables. All is peace and quiet there except for the squeaking of no one knows how many fledgling jackdaws, while the swallows over the roof beams are sitting on their nests. Their eggs may hatch out in about a week. As to our barn owls, they are nesting as usual in the unused spare-bedroom chimney, but we haven't heard any babies yet.

One small word of warning to readers who have jackdaws nesting near the house. This charming and easily-tamed bird (who learns to speak) has a weakness for anything that glitters, from a silver coffee-spoon to a ten-carat diamond. So don't leave your windows open with anything valuable lying about.

Last week we had a visitor and, one hot day (every window in the house wide open), he broke into a box of Dutch cigars and took one out, leaving the box open with four more in it and the affluent gleam of gold paper showing. When he came back the whole lot had vanished.

Later my wife had to go to the henhouse and there, on the low sloping roof just under the loft door, was the remains of the packet, all torn up, and what was left of four cigars. . . .

Doubtless Mrs Jackdaw is using that lovely sheet of gold as a bedspread for herself and her little ones. Long may they enjoy it!

A Frog has a Narrow Escape

Banshee Kilkenny Kate had been born and bred a stable cat and, when she came to us, a stable cat she remained as soon as she found out that we had horses. To her, the stable was the ideal place; there were rats and mice and friendly horses that provided comforting warmth on a cold night.

The strange thing is that our other cats very soon learned to follow her example, possibly because the stables are kept very warm (by horsepower) and horses allow cats all sorts of liberties.

This is not to say that Kate ignores human beings. She loves us and often comes in for an hour or two to warm up in front of the fire.

In cold weather all the stable cats sleep in a pile under the hay-net of my mare Blue. It is nice and dry there as quite a lot of hay falls out of the net in that corner. I've seen a cat peacefully sleeping on Patchy's broad back, he fast asleep as well.

Ann once saw Blue shoving a top-dressing of fallen hay from her hay-net over the three cats that were sleeping there.

One morning I went in with the feed to find Blue lying down in deep straw with Kate fast asleep on her back. When Blue saw me she got up with a welcoming whinny. A horse gets up front legs first and then the hind legs. There is a violent rocking motion, like a ship in heavy seas, but Kate never moved. All she did was to spread her seven-toed fingers (without any claws out), do a little balancing act while the rocking was on, then go back to sleep again as soon as Blue was on an even keel.

I have always said that a horse will never willingly step on anything living, from a mouse to a human being.

While I was putting out the feed, there were our four black cats, purring, weaving in and out of the horses' legs, rubbing against them without the slightest fear that a steel-shod hoof might come down on them. All that happened, from time to time, was that a friendly and very soft muzzle might stretch round and give a gentle shove, in case a cat was getting dangerously close, or if the horse wanted to kick out at a fly.

Later on that day my wife and I were walking round the farm on the usual tour of inspection, accompanied by Meg and two of the cats. Gretchen had stayed in the house primarily because she regards herself as a guard dog, and does not approve of cold drizzle on the last day of April.

We were fifty yards away from our new spring when we noticed that there was terrific excitement among the dog and two cats. They were leaping in the air simultaneously, the cats in deadly silence, Megan giving her horrific growls. We ran down to see what was going on. The animals were chasing and harassing a large frog.

Not wishing the frog to come to any harm, we called them off. I caught the frog and my wife took the animals away. As soon as they were decently distant, I dropped it back in the spring.

May

Meg Takes a Tumble

Our old-fashioned moss-rose is full of life, probably thanks to the bottle of rose fertilizer which Ann spreads liberally round its roots. Today it burst forth in a great blaze of sunshine; the sunlight on the back wall was six inches further south than it had been the previous day. It was going to be hot.

After an early breakfast, we sallied forth on foot for a walk with the two dogs, Gretchen the six-year-old Dobermann bitch and Meg the Rottweiler pup, now nearly twenty-five weeks old an weighing an astonishing $57\frac{1}{2}$ lbs. My wife had stipulated that she wanted a boisterous and forthcoming pup, and that is exactly what she got.

The pup and Gretchen got on marvellously together, and although they are exactly the same colour-pattern, there is an enormous difference between them. Gretchen has a long muzzle and her jowls do not hang down. In one way this is a good thing, for she only has to lift a lip to show her truly formidable teeth in a menacing snarl. She has been trained as a guard dog.

Meg on the other hand, has the mournful, sloppy-jowled face of the old English mastiff, and added to that she has the most reproachful eyes of any dog I have ever seen, with white rims underneath.

As my father would have said, she would make a marvellous deaf mute at a funeral, and so she would were it not for the fact that under that mournful, life-is-an-intolerable-burden aspect, she has a wicked non-stop sense of fun. She also is under the impression that when at home, in front of the fire, she is a lapdog. Even at less than sixty pounds, that is rather a lot of lapdog, and when full-grown at eight stone it will be even more; but three or four years will have to elapse before we have to tackle that problem.

I'd never advise any town-dweller to invest in a Dobermann

or Rottweiler unless they are prepared to pay out about three pounds a week on food and are near a good dog-training centre. They need all of this and if it is not forthcoming they can be very dangerous, not to mention destructive.

There we were on this lovely spring morning, walking up one of our single-track mountain roads, along one side of which a fast little stream was running.

Meg is a water-dog, as she should be, since Rottweilers were bred as cattle-herding dogs as far back as the time of the Roman occupation. But Gretchen, bred to guard her people against all dangers, doesn't seem to think a lot about water, that cold, wet stuff. So while Meg was happily dashing about in the stream, causing considerable anguish but no actual harm to countless small troutlings, Gretchen was stodgily plodding along to heel at my wife's side.

Suddenly around a bend there was a brilliant flash of blue at the water's edge and a kingfisher, with a three-inch trout in its beak, flew fast upstream.

Meg, with a hoarse bark, dashed after it at full speed, still in mid-stream. I pulled my dog whistle out and blew three sharp blasts. Obedient for once, she did an about-turn in the stream, and fell flat on her back in about six inches of water, with a resounding splash. By that time the kingfisher was safely home, so Meg came back, soaking us both by shaking herself.

We Nurse a Red Squirrel

An eight-year-old boy once wrote to me, asking some questions about a baby squirrel he had found and taken home. It was put on a jumper with a hot-water bottle underneath, given a little hay to eat and water to drink.

Next morning, it was found dead, some distance away from its jumper. The boy wanted to know why. The reasons for this are: first, no squirrel will eat hay; next, the water bottle may have been too hot, so it tried to move away as it was not in a box; lastly, baby squirrels will only feed on warm milk which has to be given to them with a bottle and teat as they don't yet know how to lap.

They can be tempted with broken-up nuts – hazel or walnut – but won't start eating until they feel like it. If very small, they should have warm milk in a kitten bottle and teat every four hours at least, day and night.

Recently Ann and I found a red squirrel lying half-drowned in a ditch.

It was perfectly helpless and had possibly only opened its eyes a few days previously; they are born blind and naked. Thinking we could save it, we took it home. We put it in a well-padded box on top of the oven after having dried it off, and my wife got out our own kitten-sized bottle with its tiny teat. These can be bought from almost any chemist.

Within a couple of hours it was capable of drinking, and from there on it was all plain sailing. So much so that my wife added a little wholemeal flour to the milk for added protein. By now we were keeping it in a cats' travelling basket well littered with dried peat broken up small and changed twice a day.

Within hours it was so tame we let it out in the living-room – having made sure there were no cats in the house. Squirrels are perfectly fascinating little creatures to watch at play, particularly when they sit up with their tufted ears and busy tail pricked.

With great daring the squirrel jumped down from the table on to Meg, who was lying flat on her side panting with the heat. She had just come in from a run with my wife. All that Meg did was to raise her heavy head, grin widely at the rash little thing, and let it flop back on to the floor.

Next day we decided the time had come to try to effect a release, if the youngster would call it that. We wondered whether its parents might not accept it if there were any human smell on it. But we had taken great care to handle it as little as possible, and next morning we set out for the spot where we had found it, by the stream.

Having arrived there, we opened the door of his basket, taking it up and retreating to a large gorse-bush about a hundred yards away as soon as he stepped out. Then we saw that in the middle of that thicket was a tall beech with a squirrel's drey near the top.

Invisible and out of scenting-range, we waited for perhaps twenty minutes – and then we saw the reunion.

A grown squirrel appeared at the top of the bank where ours was happily playing around. She sniffed at it, and gave it what appeared to be a playful cuff on the ear, which made it jump. Then two other small ones appeared, and that was that; they all started playing, and obviously it had been accepted. So we came out of hiding and proceeded to walk home.

As soon as the squirrels saw us they vanished into the tangle of undergrowth.

A Sheep in Distress

Three weeks ago we heard that beastly bird the cuckoo several hundred feet lower down in the valley, but haven't had one up here yet, thank goodness (as all the small birds are doubtless saying too).

For ten days we have had no rain and no gales, nothing but bright and sunny weather. All that adds up to summer, which we hope will last.

It was therefore a bit of a shock when I went down to the far paddock the other day to find a mountain ewe lying under a tree surrounded by the scattered remnants of her fleece. It is not uncommon up here in the hills to come across half-naked ewes at this time of year before the shearing. The weather is hot but it is still early, and most hill farmers have not yet shorn their flocks.

Hill sheep are notorious for getting through almost any kind of hedge or other obstacle in which wool gets pulled off by barbed wire. This used to be quite a minor industry in days of old when there was a spinning-wheel in every farm and every cottage: wool for free, it was called, but it made clothing just as good as anyone could weave with wool that had been paid for.

However, in this case, another element had entered, in the form of a marauding dog. A curious and little known (except to sheep-farmers) fact is that the best sheep-dogs have the most highly developed instinct to kill. That is why sheep-farmers always keep their sheep-dogs tethered, except when actually working or exercising under the eye of the master.

Tourists and other visitors often complain about this and call it cruelty. Sometimes they even report such cases to the RSPCA. But it is a very necessary precaution as every farmer knows.

A few years ago in this district, a dog ran amok. Before the farmers ganged up and went out (with the police) with shotguns, that one dog is said to have killed over two hundred sheep.

This ewe had been badly mauled and was lying down quite helpless, bleeding from a dozen wounds. I called to Ann to come and help, and soon we had her lying on a bed of peat in a loose box. Then I gave her an anti-tetanus shot, plus a shot of streptomycin sulphate, and sprayed each wound with antiseptic. We left her quiet for an hour, then she was given a bowl of water, a bag of hay and a saucer of whole maize.

Next time we went in she was on her feet, still a bit rocky, but looking down at an empty saucer. Sheep adore whole maize. In snowy weather it can be scattered for them on top of the snow; they never lose a single grain. The hay was untouched and so was the water; Ann ladled out another small scoop of Indian corn.

We've no idea to whom the ewe belongs because the brand on her wool was lost. But no matter; when she is well enough to travel we shall turn her loose in the lane and let her find her own way home.

We Meet a Lost Dog

As the weather was fine we decided to walk down to our local town, where it was market day, visit a friend or two and cadge a lift back to the farm from another friend who was selling some sheep.

We did not take the dogs because, although they are both highly trained and very well behaved, on a market day there are always a lot of loose dogs about with some occasional snapping and snarling.

It was gorgeous weather and before we were half-way down to the nearby village the three of us (my brother-in-law Bill was on leave from the Navy) had our coats off. In the village we made a welcome stop for a stoup of ale to cool us off, a chat with the incumbents to gather local gossip, and off we were again. The five-mile walk to the town (including the stop in the village) took us two hours.

That is not as slow as it sounds, for at least half the way consists of a hill so steep that the maximum speed (both ways) is only about two miles an hour.

We started off once our business was done, prepared to walk homeward until overtaken by the friend who was to pick us up. But about a mile out of town a young dog put paid to our plans.

We had seen it from several hundred yards away, sitting forlornly by the side of the road. A girl passed it, walking, and it bounded forward, then stopped, dejectedly returning to its stand. A Land Rover passed and it ran forward, and was left standing. Perhaps it belonged to a farmer. But then a car, going in the opposite direction, appeared, and the same thing happened.

When we got to within about fifty yards it saw us, gave a glad bark of greeting and bolted up to us.

We stopped. It gave Ann a perfunctory sniff, then came to

me, doing likewise. Then it passed to Bill. The little dog became wildly excited.

Things were getting clearer. It knew cars – therefore its owner had one or more. It was a family dog and probably thought we had been in bad company, for we smelt of Gretchen and Megan.

It semed to recognize Bill (who had never seen it before), who, seeing that it had on a new collar, stopped to read the owner's name. But of all asinine things, there was no name on the plate, no address on the dog-tag attached to the lead-ring.

A picture had formed. This was a well-loved and very well-kept dog; in fact it was a bit too fat. It was a standard Welsh sheep-dog, about a year old (give or take a month), with a white mask and throat, four white legs and a white tip to its tail. He was a male dog, otherwise Ann would have brought him home while we advertised for his owners. But as we have two pedigree bitches, it was out of the question.

All that remained was the police station. We therefore took him a mile back through the town and handed him over. All the way there he was delighted with us, probably because he belonged to a family, very much like ourselves, of at least two men and one woman; his best friend was very likely one of the men.

The police took all the details, and we left him there, the friendly little beast hating to see us go. He will be held in the local pound for eight days, and if there is no claimant we shall advertise for the owner. If no one comes forward, I am sure we shall be able to find him a happy home.

We Save a Baby Pigeon

A few days ago I had come down at the usual time to start the fire (a woodfire never goes out as long as you don't rake out too much ash), get the water boiling and make the tea for the two of us. At the same time I let the dogs and cats out but, looking out the window a few minutes later, was surprised to see both Gretchen and Meg inspecting a bird, both of them with their noses far too near its beak.

The bird was doing its best, but it was quite helpless. It couldn't get off the ground. So I went out and picked it up, taking it back to the house, followed by both highly-interested dogs who stood on either side of me inspecting it. It was, I quickly discovered, a young squab (baby pigeon if you aren't a countryman) that had very obviously been shot at when almost out of range.

One foot was broken but that would be easy to deal with. One wing had been damaged by a single pellet. The rest of the investigation had to be almost from feather to feather, to see if it had a body-wound.

By this time my wife had come down in my old dressing-gown wanting to know what had happened to her tea. So while I did that task she went on with the investigation.

When I presented her with the mug she told me that the bird was otherwise unharmed. So it was a simple matter to sever the foot, seal it and spray both that and the bone-graze on the wing with antiseptic, and then seat the bird on the back of an armchair.

I reckoned that once it had healed, enough of its leg would be left to allow the squab to take off more or less normally from the ground, where a pigeon that had lost a whole leg would probably soon fall victim to a predator.

The squab approved of its perch, straddled itself comfortably, then opened a colossal beak and loudly demanded food. Anything less like the gentle 'coo-coo, take two coos, ye fool', I have never heard – but we got the message.

It was only a matter of minutes to prepare a meal, left-over spring greens with a sprinkling of what I call human-type Swoop, an assorted mixture of cereals nicely ground, with the occasional sultana. We mixed this with a little milk and it was all greedily accepted.

The trouble with birds, both wild and domesticated, is that you can't house-train them. So we spread papers here and there, hoping for the best.

Then came the day we felt he was fit again. We took the little pigeon out into the warm morning sunshine and, having seen that there were no carrion crows about, launched him into the air.

He flew; he circled once; then he set off as straight as a die towards a patch of forestry about half a mile away.

We watched him until he checked, hovered over it for a few seconds, then dived, and we saw him no more.

All, we thought, was well.

Our New Dog Shows Her Paces

Curious, isn't it, that while rain almost everywhere ruined everybody's weekend, up here in the Welsh hills it was different. There was little sun but a thin, warm-coloured, friendly mist hung over the hilltops, and the weather was mild. We decided to have an outing.

The two of us and three dogs were in the Land Rover, banging along over the open mountain through dead heather and green gorse. At last we got to a small inn and bought some ale to go with our sandwiches, which we would eat a few miles further on at a place some would call the 'omega' of desolation. But we love it. Scattered along the hills at about three-mile intervals, you can see little whitewashed smallholdings. The rest is open mountain where sheep and their lambs roam free.

We stopped here and let out our dogs, well knowing that Gretchen and Meg would never think of running after sheep because they were both brought up as pups with lambs nearly always in the kitchen. When we let them out, they ambled off to circle in a wide arc, sniffing at everything, perfectly happy and quite at home although we were a good twenty miles from the farm.

We wanted to see how little Busy Lizzie, our new little Jack Russell, would behave on a wide-open, fenceless mountain range scattered with sheep and lambs. But Busy would have none of it; she stuck closer than a leech to Ann and wouldn't budge.

Here I should say that at the pub we had let the dogs out, before going inside. We hadn't even ordered the drinks before there came the wild wailing of a heartbroken dog. So out we went. The other two were nosing contentedly about fifty or sixty yards away, but Busy was sitting on her tail with head high, in front of the Land Rover, howling her head off and imploring it not to go without her. When she saw us she rushed up to Ann, got between her legs and stayed there. Ann picked her up, took her to the car, put her in the front and shut the door. We went back to the pub, looking back to see her grinning all over her face. She was safe. She was in the car. She knew where we were. And she was never going to let us get away. If more proof were needed that she really had been abandoned by her first owners, here it was; and we resolved that if they ever claimed her they would never get her back. First, they had let an untrained dog run free in sheep country; second, she had no identifying collar.

Now on that wild mountain we had a sign of her intelligence. She was with the other dogs, and they had approached within fifty yards of a group of ewes. The big ones took no notice, nor did the sheep. But Busy saw sheep in bulk for the first time and trotted off to investigate. I immediately whistled the recall, a long, high-pitched single note. Both big dogs immediately galloped towards us. Busy stopped and looked back, hearing the call and seeing it obeyed. Without hesitation she turned and set off towards us at full gallop.

The lesson had been learnt and for the rest of the day we had no qualms. Neither had Busy: she kept with the big ones and did whatever they did.

A Vole Comes out for a Meal

Very occasionally I write about field voles of one species or another, always in a friendly way because I like them and, where I farmed (in the hills), they are never a menace, as is their distant relative, the rat. But every time I mention them farmer friends take me to task, equating them with every other rodent as a pest. Were I farming in the lush lowlands on land worth thousands of pounds per acre, and where voles are prolific, I should think differently.

But up here, where every kind of predatory bird and animal exists, it is different. Voles are never very plentiful, and any of them that care to nest in the safety of our stone-walled buildings are welcome.

One point in their favour is that they are easily tamed and make the most charming pets. Once they are used to you they need not be caged but will nest in any little box you provide them with, as long as it is filled with hay.

We have two or perhaps three vole nests in the loose box walls, where they are perfectly safe and have a plentiful, never-ending supply of food which would otherwise be lost.

Our corn bins, as they should be, are well made of galvanized steel with close-fitting lids so that the costly contents are quite safe from rats and mice – and voles. But a small amount of waste is inevitable. Horses when eating from a manger inevitably dribble a few grains from their mouths on to the ground below, and sometimes scatter a bit more by side-swiping into it with their noses. The same applies to seeds from hay when used from a hay-net. It is not at all out of the ordinary to see a vole or two diligently searching the ground below hay-net and manger for what they can find.

The other day I had taken the hoof-clippers along to trim Rebecca's feet. She has never been shod and consequently her hooves tend to grow. If the hooves were not trimmed, they would become like Turkish slippers with turned-up toes, and make the donkey painfully lame.

One never does this sort of chore while a donkey is eating otherwise she becomes very impatient and cannot be blamed for launching out a kick or two. So I waited until she had finished her small corn ration.

Both half-doors were open so that the windowless loose box was quite light. Up in the hills where it can get extremely cold in winter, one dispenses with windows. Unbroken stone walls 22 inches thick with a stout, well-fitted door make for a warmer bedroom on the coldest nights.

Suddenly I saw a fat little vole appear on the flat edge of the manger, where Rebecca had scattered a few grains of crushed oats. Sitting on its haunches, it picked up a grain with its tiny, almost human hands and started daintily to eat. At one point it carefully examined what was left of that grain, extended a thumb and forefinger, picked something out that I could not see (probably a grain of dust), and casually chucked it to the floor. Then it continued its meal.

It must have demolished seven or eight such grains, when out of the manger itself another vole, only half the size of the first, jumped on to the ledge and attempted to snatch the last grain from under the big vole's nose.

She (I imagine she was the mother) cuffed the little one expertly back into the manger (a drop of at least eight inches) and there it stayed, quite unmolested by Rebecca. When there was no more left, they both disappeared into the peat bedding and I saw them no more. It was time to attend to Rebecca's hooves.

June

Rescuing a Calf in the Mud

One hot day we were sitting in the shade to cool off for a few minutes when we heard the bellow of a cow and a frightened reply from a calf, down at the bottom of the steep hill that leads to our east boundary.

We rushed out, got half-way down and saw it was a job for the Land Rover. We checked quickly: ten-ton towing chain, a fifty-yard length of rope and wire-cutters; everything necessary was there. We set off very carefully in bottom gear and four-wheel drive, low ratio.

In a wet winter you can't get across this land even with a tractor; on the other side of our east fence it is always a bog. There we were, near the bank, looking at a well-grown calf up to his neck in the bog and quite helpless. Also on that side, having burst through the fence, was the mother, still on fairly solid ground. Thank goodness for that. She had broken a wire which held her from getting any deeper, as it was round one foot.

Taking one end of the rope, Ann (who is nearly three stone lighter than me) went through the fence with it towards the calf, almost waist deep in the bog. Passing one end of the rope under the calf's body, she made the end fast, stood up (more than waist-deep now) and said: 'Okay!'

In the meantime I had cut the fence where the calf would be brought through and, with the pick that I keep in the Land Rover, I lowered the bank over an old stone wall along which the fence runs. Attaching my end of the rope to the front bumper, I started up and reversed very slowly. Along they came, my wife floundering about beside the calf and, when it arrived at the bank, getting it by the tail to help it over.

If this sounds cruel, it isn't. It needed help and we needed speed in case the cow tried to go for Ann. But she was a sensible cow and didn't. She turned and walked towards her part of the fence, climbed up on the bank and waited for me. While

Ann was untying the calf I cast off the other end of the rope from the bumper and tied it around the cow's horns.

She let me help her, quite patiently and obviously much relieved. I cut the wire away from her hind leg, and led her to where the calf had just been pulled through.

Ann could hardly be seen for mud and neither could the calf, but they were both on their feet and the cow started licking her offspring. We returned backwards in our tracks.

Cow and calf slowly walked up the hill and when they came to where I had previously been scything stopped for a bite of cut nettles which, having been lying for several hours in the sun, had lost all their sting. After that, we ushered them through our top gate and away they went along the narrow lane. They obviously knew where they lived, even if I didn't.

A Baby Owl Falls into our Arms

Our barn owls are becoming a bit of a nuisance in some ways.

In the spare bedroom chimney they are raising a large family of baby barn owls who snore all day long and, from about four in the morning, satiated with a night of feeding, they start snoring again.

The other day Ann climbed up the ladder leading to the granary trap-door and as her head appeared above the opening there was a great rush of wings accompanied by a ferocious noise. She was just in time to see a huge barn owl flying out through the upper door.

It was not alarming, but it was interesting; she wondered whether we now have two families of barn owls, one in the spare bedroom chimney, the other in the granary. So, the big owl having fled, she went all round the granary with an old milking-stool (she is no more than five feet tall). She examined all the eaves and there was no sign anywhere of an owl having laid any eggs.

So she concluded that this was one of the chimney owls who had just been visiting the granary in the hopes of finding a mouse or two with which to feed his ravenous brood of baby owls.

That night, as usual, we had gone outside before going to bed, putting the forecourt light on to give guidance to the dogs, and to see what sort of weather we might expect. It was cloudy and warm; the glass had dropped. We could expect rain before daylight.

What we didn't expect to see was a small cursing baby barn owl, all fluffy and looking frightfully stupid, landing in Ann's arms. Actually we did hear it slithering down the roof and were ready for it.

There it was, the stupid little thing, looking up at Ann with trusting eyes and an enormous gaping beak, asking for instant nourishment. Naturally we could do nothing in that respect, and indeed wondered what on earth we *could* do. We didn't want to keep it in the house overnight.

We got out the granary ladder which will just reach up to the roof; the other old ladder we used generally does duty for a gate. We rigged this up, having roughly contrived a hook for the old ladder to hook it over the roof-top alongside the chimney. My wife clambered up with the baby owl stuffed inside her shirt. She got on to the second ladder and started to swarm up it. She was half-way there, within three feet of the chimney, when the ladder started to slip. Although no mountaineer, I shot up the first ladder and held on to the top one, stopping its dignified descent.

'What shall I do?' she wailed.

'You're near enough to the chimney to chuck the little beast up into it,' I said. 'Try it.'

She put her hand down the front of her shirt, took the baby owl out, aimed carefully and threw it. Her exertions made the ladder slip and she descended into my arms.

We fell into a tangle on the ground, surrounded by a mass of ladders but unharmed. Before we fell I had been able to see that the little owl had been accurately aimed, falling down the middle of that chimney.

There was a certain amount of squawking, but some hours later I heard snores in the spare bedroom, and knew that all was well.

Talking to a lowland friend the other day over a mug of ale in our local, he wondered why, on selling our previous farm, we hadn't bought a civilized one about a thousand feet lower down. He enumerated all the drawbacks that go with a hill farm: cold winds up to hurricane-force in winter, cutting the fat off the backs of the unfortunate stock; torrential rains when least needed; deep snow in winter with drifts often half-way up the farmhouse, and so on.

We disposed neatly of him by saying that when a lowland (civilized) farmer comes up to the hills and buys a hill farm, one of two things happen. Either he applies lowland methods to the hills and goes bust in three years or less, or he throws all his books away and copies the methods of his neighbouring farmers. And if he makes a firm friend with the most successful, he should make ends meet. That's all there is to it.

Besides, we have our compensations; certain plants that the lowlanders do not get, such as many lovely mosses, native mini-orchids, and that little dark round fruit, variously called blueberry, bilberry, whortleberry and other names.

Around here the blueberry is lavish with its berries and many are the birds that eat it. A pigeon, the lucky thing, can fill up in a few minutes, almost to the point of being unable to take off.

We, being rather larger, are not so lucky, and the time needed to fill a quart measure is never less than an hour in the best circumstances. So far we have seen no fruit, even though some of our old stone walls are covered with the plant.

Higher up where they get more sun it might be different, and the other day we rode out, not with quart pots but to see when we could expect the crop. What soon became evident as we rode upwards was that a few weeks will pass before the blueberry crop is at its best, although there were already a few berries to be seen.

We were proceeding along a little rock-strewn gorge with walls about fifteen feet high, and ahead of us on the left, on a sloping piece of turf, I saw a hen grouse. She had not noticed us, and we stopped dead.

She was industriously pecking away, moving on several inches for each peck, which showed how long it would take even to fill a pint pot. Then we saw that she had her children with her, for all around her were tiny brown-feathered balls, pecking away (probably at imaginary blueberries) in the short mossy turf.

For a long time we watched in fascinated silence. It is a long time since we saw a grouse; indeed I had thought them extinct in these parts, but, as I have said, this is a wilder stretch of land than our old farm.

Those little things, seven or eight of them, the lot possibly weighing no more than six ounces, were having a wonderful time. Sometimes one would find himself too far away for safety, would make a smart run to his mother's side and disappear underneath her. A few seconds later he would peep out, take a look round, and emerge to continue grazing.

Suddenly a dog barked and in less than a second the mother bird and all her chicks had vanished.

We rode on, happy to think there are still a few grouse left.

A Jackdaw Flies Backwards

Today I saw a bird fly a short distance upside-down and backwards and, a split second before he landed, make a half turn to land neatly on his feet.

The way of it was this.

I've already mentioned our jackdaws, nesting here for the first time since we bought the place. We were very glad to see them and gave them all the help they needed – simply by avoiding going up into the loft where they are nesting. A very ingenious nest it is too, with two entrances; one to the outside in case the outside loft-door is shut, one to the interior of the loft. This is because in the case of a northerly gale, we always shut that door.

Lately we have discovered that they have young. At first one of the parents was always on guard in the nearest ash tree. If we let the dogs out, or went past the end of the house ourselves, a gentle hissing noise was heard, continuing until we retired. Evidently the young were taught the rudiments of flying in the loft, which has a peaked roof up to the slates with lots of beams on which to settle (and to learn to avoid in flight).

The first time we saw them in public they appeared to be quite competent little flyers, able to shoot out at full speed through the doorway and zoom up into the higher branches of the ash.

But today when I let the dogs out early for their first run, they as usual made at full gallop for the lower paddock, away from the house. Then I noticed that there were several young jackdaws on the forecourt which at that end of the house is an interesting place for a young bird. There's a henhouse with an ever-open door, well worth investigating, and the woodshed at the far end, plus a fresh load of logs on the forecourt in front of the shed. Lastly, the muck-heap – a fascinating area for exploration.

I leant up against the front door to watch in silence until one, more adventurous than the rest, flew up on to the clothes-line to where there was one genuine gypsy peg stuck, streng-thened at the fork with a silvery strip of firmly tacked on tin – a real old-fashioned gypsy peg. You don't see a lot like that nowadays. This youngster was obviously fascinated and prob-ably wanted to take it home, because jackdaws love anything that glitters.

But a puff of wind made the line sway and before that little bird knew what had happened he was hanging upside down holding on like grim death with both feet. But, alas, a stronger gust swung him wildly and, upside-down as he was he let go and made a graceful flutter down to earth, *but upside-down and backwards*!

He collected himself immediately and stalked with the exag-gerated dignity of anyone who feels that he has made a fool of himself. I let out a bellow of laughter and all the youngsters flew indignantly back to their loft.

Baby Badgers at Play

Two days before midsummer's day I got up at 3 am.

It was already dawning but I wanted to see just where, over the tallest hill in sight from the cottage, the sun would rise. The weather was perfect and in anticipation of midsummer's day being shrouded in mist, I was able to calculate where it would rise on that day. Believe it or not, it rose on the highest point of that mountain, dead in line with a very ancient beacon on the summit! Now, this cottage was built in 1720 and I liked to think the owner-builder had set his house so that the sun on 21 June rose directly behind that old beacon which had been used more than one thousand years before to give warning of invasion by the Romans.

Be that as it may. What was of more immediate importance is that I was up and about at least an hour before the sun would rise: a crepuscular but clear-as-crystal dawn.

I opened the front door quite silently – the latch and hinges are always kept well oiled so that one can go out without any noise at night.

And there, ambling along without apparently a care in the world, came a badger, closely followed in Indian file by three smaller badgers. The latter were well grown and I was not surprised because by and large the weather this spring was mild and there was more than enough for a sensible badger to get nice and fat on, such as our two loose boxes, open-doored day and night except in winter.

We always give our horses a daily ration the year round to save grass and, as they are both untidy feeders, there is generally a good scattering of barley and bran for a badger in the know, as this one undoubtedly was.

Several times in the last few years when rising early I have seen her, but previously always alone. Except, possibly, once when I saw her coming out in the half-dark. She took little

notice of me and waddled off quite unconcernedly, but ahead
I heard the noise of a heavy body (a full-grown boar can weigh
forty pounds) in hasty retreat.

This time I was unseen and unheard. On they came and I
stood like a statue in the doorway. They came up to the forecourt. Here two of the cubs started to play and presently the
third joined them. Mama sat down and had a good scratch.
The babies scampered along the forecourt, passing within three
feet of me and on towards the pile of logs at the far end.

The leader, a well-grown roly-poly on four shortish legs,
scampered up it, only to come tumbling down amidst a crashing
of fallen wood. The other two immediately set on him with
menacing growls and sundry buffets. Mama stopped her blissful
scratching and ran as fast as possible to the mêlée and dealt
out a few buffets herself. When order was restored they
marched, once again in single file with Mama in front, to vanish
inside Patchy's loose box.

For ten minutes there was a noise of slurping and guzzling
after which they reappeared, marched half-way across the forecourt until the sow either smelt or saw me. With an explosive
grunt she shot into high gear, through the open gateway to the
bottom paddock and away.

That night, last thing, my wife put out half a scoop of corn
after Patchy and Rebecca had departed to the top paddock;
yesterday morning it had gone. It may be that we have four
more beasts on the dinner-roll.

A Rare Wasp's Nest

The other day we had two friends to stay, recently married and
looking for a small place like ours in the hills, and generally
revelling in the hot, midsummer-type weather.

As we know the district very well, we went round and about
with them, looking at various deserted properties, some of

which are for sale. Some of these would need the resources of
a retired millionaire bent on making himself an ancestral dwell-
ing-place in wild Wales; vast houses with rambling buildings, all stone-built, dating from between 1600 and 1850, some
of them with the slates falling off, others with all the beams
rotting away. But there are a few in extraordinarily good condition. At the time of writing, one would have to pay £7,000 to
£10,000 for a cottage with four to five acres.

Finally we came to the last one to be viewed, not far from our
own place. Unfortunately the last owner had had to start from
scratch and applied for a grant as there was much to do inside
the house. In the contract the county insisted on bigger windows which drastically altered the character of the building.
Sometimes they also insist on raising the ceilings to come into
line with modern thought, but they did not do so in this case.

These innovations are silly. The old farmers, most of whom
built their own houses with the help of a local stonemason, knew
exactly what they were doing and made windows big enough
to see across the room in dull daylight. If reading or writing
by night, or doing early-morning milking, a tallow dip sufficed.
If in daytime you wanted to have a look at the surrounding
scenery you could go outside, have a look, and come back in
to get warm at the fire. Small windows and low ceilings both
make for the conservation of heat. Outside in winter, sub-zero
temperatures are normal.

On our search for houses we did see one fascinating thing.
In fact, it was something so rare hereabouts that I haven't seen
another in the last twenty-five years or more.

There was a pile of breeze-blocks in the yard of a farmhouse.
Some piled right way up, others on their sides with the hollow
centres horizontal. In one of these we saw a lovely specimen
of a Potter Wasp's nest right in the middle of a hollow in the
block facing us. It was backed by a solid block to the north,
but open to the south. Perfectly symmetrical, built of sand and
saliva, dome-topped with a pointed bottom, two inches long,
one and three-quarters wide, as smooth as if it had been made
on a potter's wheel – a really beautiful little artifice.

The wasp that makes it is a solitary. Having mated, she makes
her nest, and fills it with smooth (not hairy) caterpillars, which
she paralyses and drops into the nest. Having got enough food
for her baby, she lays a solitary egg, seals the little hole and

departs to make another hole and repeat the process. When the young one hatches out it feeds on the comatose caterpillars until big enough to cut its way out of the nest and fly away.

One last note. These wasps are seldom seen and are different from those of the common variety, or Picnicker's Bane, which as children we used to call the strawberry jam wasp. This one stings people.

The Potter Wasp has a slimmer black body, with two yellow half-hoops on top and three yellow bands at the rear. It too has a sting, but I have never known it to be used on human beings. Therefore it is not to be feared by picnickers or anyone else. A really nice wasp. And a truly brilliant potter.

Close Call for a Stag Beetle

A few days ago I was walking down to our east boundary over which, from our front door and window, there is a magnificent view of five ranges of rolling hills, each one a little higher than the last.

Half-way down, following an old sheep-track that has now been widened by the horses, I came across a very strange sight which reminded me of how Jonathan Swift came to write about the capture of Gulliver by the Lilliputians. He must have seen the same thing.

In the middle of the narrow track, just below an outcrop of rock making a six-inch step, lay a great stag beetle, helplessly waving its legs, flat on its back. It was surrounded by a host of ants, hundreds of them, and happily I had come on the scene within minutes of its discovery by the ants. If left to themselves, within half an hour those ants would have dismembered that great beetle (over two and a half inches long but completely helpless) and left nothing but an empty carapace. Once a stag beetle is on its back it is doomed: in no way can it get back on its feet unless helped by a friendly human being.

Nature is cruel. The weak have to bow to the strong, and in this case the massive and powerful beetle was the victim of the tiny but highly-organized ants.

I never shoot a carrion crow – or that worst exterminator of small wild birds, their eggs and fledglings, the magpie – without remembering that all predators were so created and that they also do a useful job in cleaning up dead carrion. These ants were doing their job, about to kill that immobile lump of nourishment for them and their larvae.

But I, sorry for the beetle, which had obviously fallen off the rock outcrop in the middle of the track and landed on his back on a bare surface six inches below, picked him up between thumb and forefinger. A small ant bit my finger with one end and stung me with the other but I brushed him off. There were still a dozen or more furious ants, obviously livid at being disturbed, running all over the beetle at immense speed. I blew them all off into the grass below whence they would obviously find their way home, possibly to face disciplinary action for having lost their beetle. When he was quite free of them I held him stomach-up for a moment to inspect him. His head was undamaged and none of his legs had yet been removed.

I took him to a patch of thick, short undergrowth where he could hide himself and, if so unfortunate as to fall again on the broad of his flat back, he would be able to right himself unaided by any passing human being.

A Tiger Tabby in the Ruins

From time to time in this part of the world one comes across an old track that is hardly ever used. Some of these roads, as they were surely once called, are not more than about five feet wide; so much have they been worn down by the traffic of yester-year that if you walk along them you will find the level of the fields on either side coming up to your neck.

We found one the other day, returning over the mountain (being the shortest route back home again) along a road we had not used before. At one point, where the road skirted a vertical escarpment about two hundred feet deep on one side (quite unprotected) and a practically vertical mountain on the other side, we saw an old house down in the bottom, half-hidden by a thick plantation of conifers. It looked deserted. No smoke was coming out of the chimneys and there were no electricity poles. But there might possibly be an old-age pensioner there needing a bit of help; this ruin was well off the beaten track; and there was still snow on the hills. Also, Ann wanted to have a look at it as she always hankers to buy such ancient monuments and put them back into working order.

So we went down the twisting road, very carefully, until we reached a cobbled courtyard. Sure enough, the place was deserted and we got out of the Land Rover to explore. The front door was on the latch, and in we went. First of all we went upstairs, taking care to step on the sides in case of dry rot. There were three bedrooms, no sanitation or bath (as might be expected), in one room there was an old iron bedstead.

And on the bed was a very beautiful cat, obviously a mother in milk, certainly therefore feeding a litter of kittens. She was as thin as a rail but beautiful – and very menacing. Words were not necessary; I stayed with the cat, closing the door behind Ann who pattered off downstairs, presently remaining with the remainder of our sandwiches, half a thermos of warm tea, and an old iron saucepan which she had found in the scullery. Putting the sandwiches on the end of the bed, she poured out the milky tea into the saucepan and retreated to the door again.

Very cautiously, that cat approached, sniffed, and fell to ravenously. In less than five minutes the whole lot had vanished. The cat looked at us, gave a raucous miaow, and vanished beneath the bed. She was a tiger-barred tabby, short-bodied, short-tailed and big-headed. It is said that there are no true wild cats in Wales, but I know for a fact that cats which go wild develop this striped tabby effect after several generations. So we may as well call them wild.

We left her there and returned next day with a four-pound block of dogs' corned meat, a packet of cats' crispies, and enough water to keep her going for four or five days, when we will call on her again.

Our Secret Weapon: Dirty Washing

Sometimes one gets caught napping, however experienced and however much one ought to know better.

It was thus a few days ago. Every morning either Ann or I walk the farm, checking fences and so forth, seeing that the stock is in good form or if the horses should be put into another paddock.

Once down at the bottom of the farm we found a fox's earth which was obviously in use. Having inspected the pawmarks to make sure that there were no very small cubs, we crept down in the dark of the night and blocked the earth, then poured creosote all over it.

The foxes, out hunting for food, never returned to that earth and we were content.

But one morning Gretchen had other ideas. She smelt around a bit in front of the house, made a beeline for the wall – not ten paces from the front door – and started to dig wildly, scattering weeds all over the place. Within a minute she had bared a hole at the bottom of the wall, turned to me with a triumphant yelp and paused.

I bent down and sniffed, to smell the unmistakable scent of foxes. I called her off, raked all the fresh earth smooth, and watered it well with a rose on the can.

Next morning there were the unmistakable prints of fox pads, one big and three about half size; this meant that her cubs were big and active. The family would have to be turned out. We had to render the earth unusable. They would be able to cope.

That night – or rather at about three o'clock in the morning – the alarm clock went. We got up, dressed, and went out with spades to stop up that earth. In ten minutes it was filled up and packed tight. But that was not the end.

It had to be rendered full of the smell of human beings which foxes fear. We are still without water because the spring we recently welled had to be allowed to settle down again and until we get it going properly our water comes from over a mile away in cans.

Ann therefore has a washing day only every three weeks, and there was a mountain of dirty clothing. We piled all this over the hole and that was that. I raked fresh earth our side of the entrance and left it.

Next morning there were the tracks of the family, coming up to within a few feet of the clothes, then belting off in the other direction. It had worked; they would never return.

This is a curious thing: I have known since I was a child that if a vixen has an earth on a certain farm, she will never, save under the direst conditions, kill chickens or sickly lambs on the farm she inhabits. For her hunting, she always travels a mile or two away from her home, sometimes more than that.

Within a month we shall have chickens on the place, and the mere fact that they could smell fox within yards of the house would make them nervous and reluctant layers.

Now the wall is bare except for the foxgloves along the top which we shall leave as they are so graceful. Next year the cracks between the stones will be planted with rock plants. There will be no more foxes.

July

A Cat that Enjoys a Soaking

At the moment, due to many years of neglect, the soil on our bit of land is not what you would call rich. But nettles do well on it and have really gone to town this year so that we have a magnificent crop, chin-high to me.

Nettles have many uses, You can make a very good imitation of spinach with them, but for this you have to cut them before they are more than eighteen inches high. They also make good soup. Lastly, and most important of all, livestock love them if they have been mowed and left to dry in the sun. Then the sting cannot hurt them; the spikes go limp and they can eat the leaves without stinging their lips.

I was mowing away with the scythe and had cut maybe ten square yards of the crop when I saw Puss passing by in a determined manner.

When the hot weather began we noticed that Puss had a most uncatlike habit. Everyone knows that cats can swim very well, if they have to, but that they hate to get wet and never swim unless it is absolutely necessary. When, at the beginning of the warm spell, she came in soaking wet we imagined that she must have fallen into the biggest stream hereabouts, which is at least a mile from here, a very long walk for a cat early in the afternoon.

She seemed perfectly happy, even though she is a Persian with very long fur. She lay in front of the fireless fireplace, first on one side then on the other, licking her legs. In less than an hour she was bone dry.

Every day since then – until today – she came in soaking wet on the hottest days, only up to the stomach on the cooler ones. So we accepted it: here was an exceptional cat who likes water.

But where is there any water deep enough for a cat to swim in? All the nearby streams are dried up or reduced to a trickle.

So I hung up the scythe safely in the fork of a tree with the honing-stone at its foot and followed her, at a distance of about thirty yards.

She walked straight to the other side of our well and its motor-pump. I hurried up a bit – in fact I even ran – just in time to see her tail vanishing along the overflow pipe from the first well where the water comes in. I tiptoed up to it. The tail had vanished, so I knelt down and peeped up it. The top is protected by a heavy sheet of hardboard to keep the horses from treading in it. The overflow pipe is about four inches in diameter and let in just enough light for me to see Puss lying on her side in about three inches of water. She got up and lay down on the other side. Having wet herself nicely up she got and crawled out. The entire operation had taken less than a minute. She emerged from the pipe with her usual polite little greeting to me, turned and went straight back to the cottage a hundred yards away.

So now we knew her secret. We had that rarity among cats, a water cat. And didn't she look ridiculous? As a dry Persian, she looks enormous, but as a wet one she is practically unrecognizable, more like a ninepenny rabbit than a cat.

When I got back, there she was in front of the fireplace. I lay down a few sheets of newsprint for her to dry herself on and left to resume cutting nettles for the horses.

Meg Brings Home the Sheep

The other day Ann was stripping the paint off our one remaining kitchen dresser (we originally had two, worth thirty shillings each when I bought them twenty years ago). One of them turned out to be solid oak but it was too big to get into this cottage, so I gave it to a friend. The other one is ordinary deal but stripped and newly painted will be good for a couple of hundred years.

I decided to get away from the domestic influence and set off on a five-mile ride with my mare Blue for an intake of beer and a chat with the neighbours at our local. I hadn't got but half a mile from the farm when I heard a diffident snuffle under my left stirrup and I looked down.

There was Meg, looking up at me with mournful eyes as though to say, please may I come along?

Well, why not? So along she came. We were on one of our single-track mountain roads and there was little traffic, but every time a car overtook or passed us Meg got on my inside, immediately getting back into the middle of the road for my protection when it had passed.

We arrived at out local where Meg lost no time in making friends with the pub pup about one-tenth of her size, for Meg, then eight months old, already weighed not far from a hundred pounds. But she is gentle and can play with a half-pound kitten without ever hurting it. Then, remembering her responsibilities, she went outside to keep a watchful eye on Blue, tethered in the yard.

The lovely thing about these Rottweilers is that for two thousand years at least they have been civilized. They are enormously intelligent; they are gentle with animals; but when necessary, they are truly formidable guard dogs. Ever since we brought Meg home as an eight-week-old pup, I have wanted to train her as a cattle dog, but we have no cattle.

On the way home, rounding a very sharp U-bend, we came across a couple of newly-shorn ewes, each with a lamb. One lamb was in dire distress. Its near hind leg was grievously wounded, though one could not tell how. The hip was dislocated but there was also a deep wound, from near the tail to the hock, and there were flies about.

I said 'Quiet, Meg, and on guard', gently turning Blue to the sheep. Meg looked up at me with her doleful eyes, went round to the right and quietly turned them into the road ahead of us. Meg has had no training in the handling of stock, and yet for the mile-long ride home, she never put a foot wrong. She kept those two ewes and two lambs on the road quietly and without any fuss, this side, that side, but always ahead.

Before we got to our farm there were two cars behind us, locals who would never dream of forcing through. When we arrived home, Meg turned the sheep in left and actually stabled them, while the farmers in their cars congratulated me on having such a herd dog. I didn't tell them that Meg had never had any previous training.

Thereafter it was a simple matter to clean up the wound, give all the sheep a feed and leave them in overnight. Next morning we turned them out and I knew that I had a dog suited either for sheep or cattle.

How Hannibal Beat off an Intruder

Up here in the hills there are certain problems in keeping your own poultry.

To begin with, there are literally hundreds of foxes in a five-mile radius from this farm, and foxes dote on poultry. Also (but very occasionally) you get the aged badger who has lost nearly all his teeth. These animals generally work by night and are very intelligent about breaking into a henhouse. By day there is always the hazard of carrion crows (and I don't mean rooks) flying over the top of the chicken-run and eating the eggs. The same can be said for magpies and occasionally jays, both of which belong to the crow family.

We inherited what could be called a henhouse and for want of time decided to use it, providing a dry floor, weather-tight walls and ceiling, with covered-in laying pens. As to the free range, we reckoned that forty yards by twenty yards would be plenty as a permanent run for up to ten chickens, netted all round and over the top.

As the whole thing would be within forty yards of our bedroom window, if we ever hear the alarm – given by Gretchen and Meg who both sleep with us – all I have to do is to open the window with torch in one hand and gun in the other, and read the riot act.

This procedure dates from time immemorial. When my grandfather was young, he would have leaned out with a lanthorn and blunderbuss, in a flannel nightgown and night-cap.

'This blunderbuss is double loaded with a quarter of a pound of old horseshoe nails: advance at your peril!' he would have yelled.

So far this has not happened here but it could any night, which is why it is always wise in remote hill farms to have your chicken -run in full view of the bedroom window – and within shotgun range.

We decided on Rhode Island Reds because they are good layers, handsome birds, and better at looking after themselves than some other breeds. We got seven pullets and a really good rooster who immediately had all our attention. We named him Hannibal.

Hannibal is extremely aggressive to outsiders and, when I took possession of him (holding him gently in my arms), he tried to peck my eyes out. When we turned him into the compound with his seven wives the first thing he did was to inspect every inch of it. The ample run was netted all round and over the top, which had his approval. Then he went into the henhouse and inspected every part of it. Everything according to him was hunky-dory, particularly the feeding arrangements.

That evening, an hour before sundown, pandemonium broke out. Forth we rushed, dogs and all, to see a magpie walking across the top net. Hannibal was fly-jumping up and down from inside, and I'm almost certain got a peck or two at the intruder while making the most menacing noises.

When we ran from the front door, yelling all the bad language we knew, away flew that horrible black-and-white pest, and I don't think he'll be back again. Hannibal strutted proudly up and down in his version of a war dance, while his adoring wives applauded him with all their hearts. The following day we had our first five beautiful eggs.

A Trapped Lamb

There's a wild piece of mountain about six miles north-east of us which we love – and that includes the dogs.

Some people who see it for the first time visibly shudder and turn to us: 'How anyone can possibly live in a place like this beats us. A desolation of desolations.'

Well, there's no accounting for taste, is there? But it's too far to walk there and back on a hot day. So we go in the Land Rover: Buzy Lizzie in the middle seat between us, always with her front paws either on my wife's legs or mine (depending which side she finds more interesting), standing up and eagerly gazing out of the windscreen or side window. Meg and Gretchen stand in the back with their heads alert, Gretchen's head on my right shoulder for support (quite heavy sometimes) and Meg on the left with her head over my wife's shoulder.

Part of our road skirts the side of a nearby mountain, about half-way up it. On the left is a sheer drop of several hundred feet; on the right, a steep rise to the summit. The road is only eight feet wide all the way up. As it is a one-in-seven rise with no passing bay all the way, it can be tricky, even though they have recently put a stout steel guard on the precipice side. Near the bottom there is a recently installed cattle grid for cars beside the farm gate so that drivers don't have to open the gate and shut it behind them on what can be a very steep slope, often covered with ice in winter.

When we came in sight of the gate, we could see that something was wrong. Two sheep were standing by the grid, one on each side. The one on our side was frantically bleating. The far one appeared to be a ram who had somehow got over to the wrong side.

We knew where they belonged because they had recently been shorn and newly marked with the owner's brand. In the middle of the grid was stuck a large fat lamb in a fearful state yelling his head off.

We stopped below the cattle grid alongside the gate and I opened it for my wife to get through with Megan. Gretchen stayed with me while Meg made a quick scoot up the mountain so as to get back to the ram on the up-side and turn him back through the gate.

My wife just stood there and waved an arm once. In a jiffy the ram was on our side without ever a curse from him or a bark from Meg. Meanwhile, Gretchen sat quietly by my side without a murmur.

Then my wife went to the grid and both dogs got down the road so that the ram and ewe would not get too far. My wife walked across the grid to the lamb before it could disappear into the pit beneath, pulled it out and put it down on the road.

It shot away to its mother and next moment its tail was wagging ecstatically as it took a nourishing drink.

We started the car, went through the gate, shut it and went on. Our last glimpse of the sheep was three backsides with tails wagging, running down the hill, the smallest backside safely in the middle.

We Rehouse some Swallows

A few weeks ago, our swallows, which arrived late this year, reared their first brood and were teaching them to hunt for food.

Our telephone wire comes into the house at the granary end, over the stables, the last post being our nearest ash tree which is almost dangerously near the house. From the last insulator (bolted into the tree) to its entry into the house is a stretch of six or seven yards, which the baby swallows, quickly tiring after several minutes of frantic swooping, diving and turning this way and that chasing flying insects at full speed, find very useful for resting tired wings and getting their breath back.

Often, in the first week that they were learning to fly, you would find seven or eight of these little birds sitting in a close line on this wire until one of the parents, thinking they had had sufficient rest, would swoop by almost brushing them, with loud tweets. Off the little birds would go for another few rounds.

When they rested on the wire we could walk right up to within a couple of paces of it, and the little birds would calmly sit there looking at us, not in the least disturbed. They regarded us like cats and dogs, or even the horses, as belonging to the place. And once, when my wife squeaked at them, they all squeaked back in chorus.

This has become a daily routine. Whenever she goes out in the morning, if they are on the line she squeaks good day at them, and they politely reply, with added dialogue which, without quite understanding, she answers.

Now the swallows are rearing their second brood. Three days ago Ann came into the house in some distress, telling me that one of the nests had fallen – or been pushed by a cat – to the floor; that one swallow was dead and that two others were alive and apparently quite well though hungry.

I went along with her and there was the nest lying shattered on the ground directly under the wide shelf below the roof on which it had been built. It had been too near the edge and had overlapped; this is not the first time that I have seen it happen. It was certainly not the work of cats. Two tiny survivors were comfortably crouched together in a bit of sacking on the box where Ann had put them. And now, what to do? Knowing how very sensitive many small birds are about their nests, there had to be a quick remedy – but would it be acceptable? One could but try.

Ann ran down to the larder and finally returned with a wide dull-blue plastic bowl with a rim not more than a couple of inches high. Accommodating the fledglings in it, on top of their piece of sacking, she put it on the top of the wall, so it did not overhang. There it would be safe, provided the parents approved. All this time they had been flying fast in and out of the loft, squeaking madly, sometimes almost brushing our heads with their wings. We left them, hoping for the best.

Next day Ann went up early to hide herself at the far end, underneath the water tanks, keeping as quiet as possible. Half an hour later she came down to report that twice the parent-birds had returned to the nest with food, and as soon as they flew out the little ones resumed squeaking.

Soon they will start to fly, because they were already fully fledged, except that their tails had not yet grown out more than half an inch.

We shall leave the nest there, nailing it firmly down before they return next year. Indeed, it might be an idea to do the same for the other nesting swallows. It will at least prevent another similar accident or worse, a far more lethal one.

To the Rescue of a Mountain Pony

A few years ago, while taking some friends out for a ride through one of the forests which are plentiful around here, we came to a treacherous place, steep and thickly planted with spruce.

I told the riders to keep in my tracks and not diverge a foot either way, as there was a very nasty bog half-way up the hill. But one girl preferred to take her own way and immediately her horse was sunk belly-deep. It took us twenty minutes to get her out and when I asked her what she thought she was up to, she replied through her tears that she thought I had been joking; surely you couldn't have a bog on a mountain top? Well, you can, as she learned to her cost.

Although we have been at our new farm for almost a year it could take ten years before we really know the countryside around within a five-mile radius.

A thin drizzle was falling the other morning when Ann and I went out with the horses and I recalled that little incident.

The hill we were crossing had very little soil on its sides and there were great expanses of rocky outcrop across which no sensible person would try to ride. They are almost as slippery as ice, particularly when they are wet.

In such cases one always follows a sheep-track, which sometimes makes for slow travelling, as they twist and turn, and are seldom more than about six inches wide.

But it is better to be safe than sorry, and I suppose we were making two or three miles an hour, but the white-faced native mountain sheep are very wise and know their country. We arrived at the flattish top, still following our little track, when we saw something rather sinister about a quarter of a mile ahead.

A small boy was waving and yelling to us, and we could see the head of a pony and about half its body beside him.

We speeded up after finding another sheep-track leading roughly in his direction, and were soon on the spot.

He was a mountain boy and we were surprised, as we made preparations for getting the pony out, that he should have got into such a predicament. He explained that he knew the country and was proceeding quite happily when out of a thick clump of marsh grass a big dog fox had suddenly dashed. His pony had shied violently, and next moment was elbow-deep in the bog.

The pony was small, light and intelligent. My wife and I always carry a tie-rope rather than a Hackamore on our mounts, and by joining the two together we had a fifteen-foot rope. I tied this into the side of my surcingle while my wife put her surcingle around the pony's girth. She got on one side of the pony (the drier side), while they boy, who was already soaked, got on the down side.

I mounted Blue (who had done this sort of thing before) and gently took the strain while my wife and the boy lifted as well as they could. The pony knew what was wanted from him; he didn't panic or waste any strength, but quietly helped to free himself. And in five minutes he was on dry land again, shaking huge clots of dark-coloured mud all over us.

A Nocturnal Arrival

Since buying and living in this little farm several fascinating developments have occurred.

One of them – interesting certainly but in its small way disastrous – was the drying up of Pantffynnonlas, 'the Blue Well in the Hollow', reputed never to have run dry in all its existence. Well, maybe so; but nearly ten weeks ago it did just that. All our drinking and cooking water has to be brought daily from five miles away, while water for the stock comes from a little nearer when the rainwater tubs run dry.

Also interesting and fascinating is the fact that now, for the first time in twenty-five years, the wildlife on the place is slowly increasing because of good husbandry.

Last night something really exciting happened. It was pitch dark with a heavily overcast sky, but was not raining, and Ann went out to get a kettleful of rain water for the washing-up. To do this she switched on the forecourt light.

Ann hadn't even closed the front door when she called to me to come running. Out I went, to find her in a state of great excitement, and I asked her what was the matter.

'There's a bat about,' she said; but it was some time before we saw it again. It fluttered past the light, not more than a foot or two away from it, obviously taking flying insects that had been attracted to the light, and, so it seemed, making quite a feast.

Almost certainly it was a pipistrelle or common bat, the smallest of its species in this country, and an amazingly active flyer. Although so small it has a wingspan of between eight and nine inches, and we were more than delighted to see it.

One of the saddest results of the assassination of the rabbit population over twenty years ago is the fact that in many districts the bat population seems to have been very largely liquidated too; the reason for this is that members of the stoat family from the polecat down seem to have learned to climb trees.

Se we very much hope that this small member of the *Vespertilionidae* tribe has found a safe dormitory under our roof, and will raise a family next year.

A Donkey Comes to Visit

When I get up on summer mornings, Rebecca and the horses are usually down in the east paddock, grazing. But when Ann is about to come down, first of all the dogs jump up, quite frantic to see her, and then Rebecca, although she may be a hundred or more yards from the house, knows that Ann is coming downstairs, lifts her pretty head and lets out a shattering bray.

In a few seconds comes an answering bray. This belongs to a very small grey donkey (a jenny) who lives, as the crow flies, about half a mile away, although by road it is a mile. The house lies in a dip and we can't see it. But the bray carries very clearly and we nearly always hear it. We realized long ago that this little donkey answers because she is lonely and would like a little company, please.

Last Sunday morning, when Ann came down, Rebecca as usual let forth her bray, and immediately both she and Patchy came galloping up to say good morning. Then, almost immediately, came the answering bray of the little grey donkey, not a hundred yards from the cottage; and within a minute or less there she was, standing at the drive gate, yelling to be let in. Ann opened the gate and the stranger made much of her before trotting down the forecourt to greet our two.

And here was an interesting point. If a strange horse had come up unasked like that, Patchy (who is very possessive about Rebecca) would have objected strongly. But in the case of this little jenny he was all smiles.

Naturally, when feeding, we also had to put out a feed (mixed oats, cornflake and bran) for the little grey, and she tucked in happily, not to say greedily.

After that it was only left for Ann to put a halter on our visitor and lead her back to her home. The owners were not there, but they had evidently left the gate open. What interested me was the fact that their donkey, although she knew the direction of our cottage in a straight line as noise travels, had to take a twisty road with a crossroad near the end to get to us. But she had known how.

August

An Intruder Wakes Me Up

We were both fast asleep and had been for some time when all hell broke out in the living-room below, where our dogs sleep in front of the fire.

I leaped out of bed and rushed down the staircase with a powerful torch in one hand and a gun in the other. I opened the living-room door so that the dogs could help, then flung open the front door, which is never locked at night, and ran out.

Curiously, neither of the dogs showed the least interest, and after I had delivered the standard old challenge of 'Stand and deliver, this blunderbuss is loaded!' there was a dead silence outside.

Feeling rather silly I returned to the house and there were the dogs comfortably settled down on the mat in front of the dying fire.

Having got back into bed I told Ann what had happened. We concluded that Gretchen had had a nightmare, got up yelling, and that had alerted Meg.

At eight o'clock the next morning I turned on the radio for the news and as I did there was a mighty rushing as of a wind from Heaven over my head.

I ducked quickly and next moment there was a bang over the bookcase as two antique candlesticks and a candle-trimmer with snuffer on its little salver all clattered to the tiled floor, along with a nine-pounder pom-pom shell-case that we use as a vase.

Ann also ducked wildly as a barn owl smacked into the wall just over her head. The owl, about half-grown, hopped quickly across the floor and took station in a corner of the bookcase. There it stood straight up and glared at us all.

In all the years that I have known animals, I had never seen a barn owl at such close quarters. Two great eyes glared at me from a perfectly white heart-shaped face. When you see these great birds flying at dusk or in the light of the moon, they appear to be absolutely white, yet they are not: there is a lot of brown on them.

They used to inhabit the granary over the stables, but when we re-floored the barn we also repaired the door. And although we made an owl-door for them, by that time they had nested in our north chimney, which is never used.

Barn owls do not build nests, but in this case they have taken over all the jackdaw nests that have been built into that chimney for many years. And now one of the young owls had evidently mistaken our living-room chimney for his.

These chimneys are wide enough for a small boy to scramble up and sweep them, with foot-holds on either side to make it easier.

The owl must have landed spread-eagled on top of a dying fire and frightened the dogs. But, having landed unhurt, he made the best of things. He slept in the bookcase all day, and when he woke up at twilight, we opened the window. Away he flew, silently, into the night.

Our Dogs Race for a Rabbit

With a chill north wind blowing, this can hardly be called a typical summer's day only a fortnight after official midsummer. In fact I put on my warm winter waistcoat before venturing out to see what Ann and the dogs were doing.

It was a grim landscape altogether, like a bleak November day save for the fact that there are leaves on all the trees.

Ann had got the water-supply pump going and brought up an armful of young ragwort, which is deadly poison to horses when growing and even worse when mixed with hay. It will go on the fire as soon as one is built. She was also gathering wild flowers to fill the little earthenware bowl (made within three miles of this house) in our bedroom. There is nothing more beautiful than a bowl of wild flowers, grateful things that last for ages, to grace a window.

Meanwhile the three dogs were having a grand time racing around the little paddock. All, that is to say, save Gretchen, who has established herself as my own personal guard dog. Seeing me, she put on her OAP's walk and hobbled stiffly up to me. I knew exactly what she meant, for at times (to infuriate Ann) I put one on myself.

But hers was for a different purpose. She meant, Master, 'tis bloody cold; will you take me into the house where, without a fire, it isn't much better. But at least it isn't quite so draughty as outside.'

I saw her point and returned her to the sitting-room, leaving her in front of the empty fireplace looking back at me in a very reproachful manner. Poor old thing, she is beginning to feel her age.

I returned to the paddock to where Ann was pulling up docks, while Meg and Busy Lizzie were bouncing about all over the place quite unconscious of racing clouds, wildly waving trees and draughts galore. My wife was nearing the end of her dock patch and I was thinking of pulling up a couple while they lasted, just to show willing, when suddenly, Busy gave her hunting yap and shot off at right angles towards the remaining docks, followed of course by Meg who, with her superior weight and equal speed, tried to make a right-angle turn and, of course, went sprawling on her side.

So Busy got there yards ahead, sprang a young rabbit, made another right-angled turn and overtook it at full speed, hurling her body on top of it and scoring a bull's-eye. Having pinned it, she looked back at us, grinning widely and gave her other yap demanding attention – as if it were necessary! Ann walked forward and took the rabbit from her. She was not biting it, just holding it down with her forepaws.

Ann picked it up, gave it to me, and went to the house, calling to the dogs. I had hidden the rabbit under my coat and waited until they had vanished, Ann carrying Busy and making much of her.

Then I went into the lane where I had previously seen what might well have been that particular rabbit popping into a thick growth of gorse on the wide verge, and turned it loose.

It popped into that haven and doubtless in the next few seconds told mama all about the horrible experience.

Puss Goes Diving

We decided recently it would be an ideal day for gathering stones for the forecourt wall that Ann has been building in her spare time.

It is fascinating to think that the old tumble-down wall we were taking the stones from must have been built in the seventeenth century.

We know this because, growing out of the middle, and still in perfect condition, are three enormous ash trees, six feet wide, which a tree specialist friend of ours dated at over three hundred years old.

Many of these walls are far older, reaching back to 2,000 BC or earlier, and none of the stones are quarried. They were just picked up off the surface of the land, mainly by the wives and children of the old farmers. And we were filling the Land Rover with these stones, some of the big ones weighing up to a hundredweight.

All around us the dogs were fooling about, taking care not to step on any of the many cats that were carelessly scattered all over the place. All, that is to say, but Puss, doyenne of the cattery, the swimming cat who eats tadpoles but is a very good mouser as well. She was conning the broken-down wall. I was just about to tell her that she would find no tadpoles there when she pounced. Next moment up she came with a beautiful little lizard in her mouth.

But Ann too had seen, and pounced almost simultaneously, catching Puss by the scruff of her neck. Puss, astonished that a mistress could commit a five-foot leap as fast as she herself, opened her mouth and the lizard dropped neatly into Ann's hand.

It was a common lizard but greener than most (presumably on account of the very green grass growing along the top of the wall) and not more than three inches long; evidently a young one. It was quite unhurt. So after a short consultation Ann pointed its blunt little head towards a nice opening between two stones into which it vanished.

We put two protective stones that Puss would not be able to move in front of it, leaving sufficient room for the lizard to get out. As we had seen another lizard, disturbed by our nefarious vandalism, we bundled up the cats on top of that load, went home and shut them up, then unloaded the stones. After a drink of cider, we returned for another load and so passed the rest of the day without further aggravation for the inhabitants of the ancient wall.

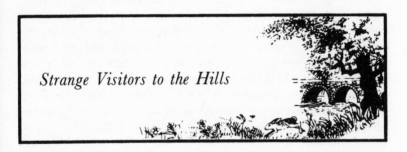

Strange Visitors to the Hills

The other morning I saw something I had never seen in my life before. There, on the back paddock fence not four paces from the kitchen window, was a very active bird, sitting for a few seconds on the fence, then shooting down to the ground, picking something up and returning to the fence.

Several times this was repeated. Obviously, it was an insect-eater. It had a beautiful reddish chest, with a brilliant white cap, a dead-black throat and the red shading to buff on the underside.

It was perfectly lovely, but I couldn't put a name to it until I looked through my *Observer's Book of Birds*, a very useful little book that fits into a pocket. I have never been what is called a bird-watcher because it is one of those static occupations like sit-fishing that I have never had much time for. This is possibly why I had never seen a redstart, as this definitely was, up in Wales before. As a summer visitor I had always imagined it to be confined to the warmer, southern part of the country. But here it was high up in the hills of south Wales.

I told Ann the news. I'm not quite sure if she believed me or not, but anyway she showed great interest and went to the kitchen to look.

Suddenly Ann's excited face appeared in the kitchen doorway and she beckoned. In I crept, and there it was again, in exactly the same spot that I had first seen it, a very beautiful thing. Then she squeezed my arm and pointed across the paddock.

'There's his mate,' she whispered, and I saw, flitting from a branch to the bark of the trunk, where he pecked enthusiastically, *another cock!*

This was really something. Almost certainly there would be a couple of hens lurking nearby.

After breakfast it was time for Ann to take the dogs for their usual walk. She was determined to keep both dogs quietly at heel until well away from the garden where we believed the redstarts to be nesting, probably in holes in the old stone wall. As soon as they went out of the front door, however, they saw a cock bird perched on the drive gate. Gretchen was as good as gold and stayed behind Ann's leg, but the more ebullient Meg saw the brightly-coloured visitor and immediately started to bounce forward on stiff legs.

But the bird did not take fright. He waited until Meg was within three feet of him, then performed an impressive vertical take-off and alighted on a branch some twenty feet up. There he sat until Meg had finished her barking and bouncing, and Ann opened the gate. Only then did the redstart return to the old garden, to his still unidentified home there.

Tom Gets Trapped in a Tree

Cats, like ourselves, come in all shapes and sizes, particularly as regards ancestry. Cleo, the China cat with a very long Ming

pedigree, is not a hunter. She reclines at ease and waits for
minions to supply her wants. The other two she-cats, Puss and
her daughter Tartan (Tarty for short), both Persians, are the
hunters.

Thomas the tom-cat, black and obviously sired by a descend-
ant of our own strain of polydactyls, is the son of Cleo, therefore
with conflicting ancestry. He would dearly love to be a hunter.
Physically he has everything but mentally, alas, he takes after
Cleo in some ways. He is boisterously affectionate, whereas his
mama is very genteel about showing her approval of anybody
or anything. Although quite affectionate, the most you will ever
get out of her is a discreet purr.

Tom, on the other hand, is all over us and loves to lie on
my wife's lap or mine. But since Busy Lizzie the Jack Russell
came to live with us, if she wants to lie there (she's quite light)
she doesn't think twice about turfing Tom off.

When it is dinner-time the cats all know it. Cleo will have
spent the day either on a lap or in front of the fire. The other
three (unless it is raining buckets) have been out all day and
come dinner-time there they are, all sitting on the window-sill
waiting to be let in. After dinner, barring foul weather, Puss
and Tartan want out-for-the-night but not Tom. He and his
mama sleep in the kitchen.

A few nights ago he did not come up for dinner.

It was already dark but we didn't worry much because,
although it looked like rain, we knew that if Tom was out cat-
ting he would spend the night quite comfortably in somebody's
barn or stable whispering sweet nothings to his lady love.

Next morning, however, he was still absent. So, after break-
fasting the others (and ourselves), we all sallied forth, first along
the lane to see if some nocturnal driver might have run him
over. But he was nowhere there.

Suddenly, from the other side of the farm, barking broke out.
We were wondering what had happened when Busy Lizzie
appeared at the gallop. Bouncing about, she conveyed to us
that she wanted to be followed, and this we did.

About a hundred yards down on the other side of the house,
the other two dogs were standing at the foot of an old tree long
since killed by ivy.

I have been meaning to cut it down for ages and, whatever
the road to hell is paved with, failure to carry out my good

intention might have been the death of poor Tom. For there he was, imprisoned between two thick and twisted trunks of ivy, all contracted round the midriff and looking like a feline egg-timer. Ann ran to the house and soon came back with the axe. A couple of accurate swipes cut through the ivy-trunks and, having untwisted the ivy, Thomas fell thankfully unhurt into Ann's arms.

Thomas led the way up to the house followed by Ann and the dogs plus Puss and Tartan, who had joined the throng.

I gave a casual swipe with the axe at the base of the tree, meaning to cut it down there and then. But that first bash went right through the foot-thick trunk. It was completely rotten. Down it came, narrowly missing me.

There had been wind during the night and it was a good thing it had not fallen while Tom was stuck in it, or he would have been squashed flat. But all was well and he was able to join the rest of the family.

I Round Up Some Strays

The other day I was returning from town with the dogs in the Land Rover.

At this time of year Meg is especially useful, for the autumnal sheep-sales will soon be starting and already there is a certain amount of movement along our narrow mountain roads.

It can happen that if the Land Rover or any other car meets a few strays on the road, the sheep will run for miles before the car without giving it a chance to pass.

In our case, if we meet such a bunch I stop the car, get out and if necessary cross a fence to get ahead of them, then walk on in whatever direction I know their gate to be with Meg coming along behind or in the front as the case may be.

Soon we came across such a bunch of sheep and from the mark on their sides I knew where they came from, half a mile ahead where the road was very narrow. Stopping the Land Rover I sent Meg ahead to hold them. Driving right up into the verge so as not to block the road, I left the car there and followed the sheep. Meg kept a wary eye for any gap in the hedge or open gate.

Presently we got near the gate through which they had to be turned into their field. So, warning Meg to hold them, I walked carefully by and opened the gate. Then I sent Meg further along the hedge of the field so that she would be able to get back into the road behind them.

By now they had straggled back about a hundred yards, Meg stopping every few yards to see whether she was still behind them. When she was past, she neatly jumped the three feet hedge into the road and I gave her the sign to come along.

Quickly opening the gate I went back to the road to turn the sheep in. On they came, quietly herded along by our Rottweiler. Without any hesitation they turned into the field and happily galloped away wildly wagging their uncontrollable tails.

Up here we do not dock our sheep. Tails produce valuable wool as well as fat on which the sheep may live when food is scarce.

After shutting the gate, going back to the Land Rover, and getting going again, I gave Meg a Cornish pasty I had bought in town as a just reward for her beautiful, instinctive sheep herding.

Chaffinches Scare off an Owl

Backend has come. There's no doubt about that.

The swallows who, according to the sages, should be thinking of returning south to warmer climes in mid-August, and doing so by the end of that month in a normal year, have this year already vanished from the hills. An early backend could mean an early winter followed by an early spring.

A little happening two days ago makes me wonder more. In all the years that I have been writing about birds I have seldom mentioned the short-eared owl. It is not a common owl, occasionally nesting here, but more often a winter visitor to Britain. The one I saw (in broad daylight, which is common with this particular owl, who hunts both by day and by night) was busy turning over small stones.

On many fields up here these small flat shaley stones are common and they afford a cool resting ground for worms and countless beetles, plus other grubs.

I was standing on the other side of one of those rounded banks that long ago was a stone wall. Little by little, the top stones fall and the wall becomes low and rounded. The wind brings dust which becomes earth. Things grow on it, including local bushes such as rowan, hazel and so on until nature turns it into what, with little help on the farmer's part, becomes an efficient hedge.

The owl hadn't seen me. It was very busy and highly profitably so. Each stone, about as big as a half-sandwich, yielded several worms of various sizes, a beetle or two and other grubs as well.

Suddenly the owl looked up, standing as though on tiptoe, looking towards my wall-hedge about thirty paces away. Then it took off towards it, flew about ten yards and was just coming down on something when with furious screeches it was attacked by half a dozen or so chaffinches.

Then I saw what had attracted it. There was a fledgling (chaffinch, obviously) banging about on the ground, making futile attempts to fly. But every three inches of altitude it gained, it immediately lost. However, that didn't matter. Owls never go looking for trouble because usually they don't have to. And in this case – well, what matters one small fledgling when the belly is already stuffed with worms, beetles, leather-jackets, wire-worms and such like delicacies. Not worth the couple or so feathers that I've already parted with, said the owl to himself, and departed at full speed. Alighting about fifty yards away, just about to turn over an inviting stone, he was again attacked by the angry squad, now increased to what looked like a dozen. Then he departed in earnest and I saw him no more.

The chaffinches returned and dispersed, all but three of them, obviously the parents and a ma-in-law, roundly berating the infant, but, at the same time, herding him carefully towards the wall.

I wondered whether the short-eared owl was resident. I hadn't seen one up here for four years, and that was in the middle of winter....

September

Our Field-Mice
Get in a Tangle

Going into the larder this morning I was astonished by a sudden flurry around a deep little saucer of duck-grease – the previous day we had shared a roast duck and, as everyone knows in the country, both duck- and goose-grease make a very valuable liniment for rubbing into a roupy chest in winter.

For the moment all was a confusion of long-tailed field-mice. One, in its efforts to get to safety, jumped up off the slate slab, caught hold of a length of binder-twine hanging down from a roll on the next shelf up. It had climbed at least three inches with grace and agility when the whole roll came down, landing on top of it and two other small mice that had been looking up, doubtless awaiting their turn.

The mother mouse was completely unperturbed. There appeared to be two more mice in the gathering because one nose and two bright eyes were peeping at me from round the side of a cider bottle, and another such semi-profile was peeping over the top of a Marmite jar.

Everything was quiet. I had succeeded in not laughing. Mama – evidently accustomed to my daily appearances – continued slurping up her grease very neatly. The two who had fallen to the floor had by now disentangled themselves from the roll of binder-twine and were nowhere to be seen, until they reappeared on the slab and joined mama.

The Marmite jar mouse had jumped up, and was sitting on its top, grooming his long whiskers with delicate little hands, assessing the situation and concluding that there had been nothing to worry about. Having finished his whiskers he rejoined the half-circle round the saucer, sniffed at the luscious grease but refrained from eating any more. One small mouse appeared to be in the throes of hiccups, which nearly lifted him off the slate table-top every time.

Old Welsh country houses, farmhouses and even cottages like

ours, particularly in the hills, all have these slate slabs, supported two feet off the floor on heavy mortared brick pillars, round three sides of every larder. They are wonderfully cool in summer.

We never upset these long-tailed field-mice, nor the voles. Both species are common here, but never in too great quantities. We like them because not only are they very graceful, but they are easily tamed once they realize that human beings mean them no harm.

I had forgotten what I had come to get, so I quietly closed the door on the little family and left them to it. Anything else that they may have liked to sample was quite safe either in tins or glass jars, all with stoppers on.

A Furious Robin
Starts a Fight

Some weeks ago I mentioned that our small-bird population had departed to lower altitudes, where they could find the river and larger streams still holding a bit of water. All that remained with us were two pairs of blackbirds, one pair of thrushes (very much a rarity up here) and two little families of wrens. There was also one robin and we think he must be the one who made a point of tapping on the window and demanding entrance (with a meal, please) during the deeper frosts last winter.

They say that it is bad luck to permit entry to a robin. That we regard as nonsense. My first memory of a robin in the house occurred when I was three, since when there have been many; and I think I have had better luck than perhaps I deserved for most of my life.

Then, two or three days ago, I got up reasonably early and, on looking out of the living-room window, was astonished to see birds all over the place, and a big variety of them too. Very conspicuous were a pair of bullfinches with three large children, the usual agglomeration of chaffinches, possibly rather more than the usual pied and grey wagtails, two or three sparrows (I would have expected more) and three robins.

As they had been absent for so long, I put out some corn and, from force of habit after weeks of doing so for our remaining birds, filled the water-dishes.

To my astonishment they deserted their corn and crowded round the dishes, not for drinking but to bathe.

And then trouble started. The resident robin who had been with us all summer attacked with fury not one robin or one bird but the whole lot. They scattered, astonished, and suddenly there he was, alone in the middle of a ring, surrounded by what he considered were awestruck birds.

The two adult robins that had spent the drought by the riverside flew savagely at him and the battle commenced. All I saw was a blur of red and brown with plenty of noise and what I surmised was a cry or two of encouragement from the other birds spectating. But it was not to last for long. A cruising buzzard, attracted possibly by the noisy scene, floated gently down on motionless wings and swooped slowly over them. Immediately there was a frantic scattering as the entire audience sought the safe sanctuary of the row of blackthorns along the nearest stone wall.

No buzzard would try to breach such a dangerous thicket. As for the robins, our permanent resident shot round the corner of the house behind the garage, where he lives, chased by the others.

I went out to send off the buzzard perched, as I had thought he would be, on top of the roof. Within two minutes of returning to the house the birds had come back, some to eat, others to bathe.

The non-resident robins returned too but this time all was peace; no more tempers. I went out to the back to scatter some food for the defeated robin; at least he had one friend.

A Badger who Called at Dawn

It is quite widely believed that both foxes and rabbits occasionally make use of a badger's set. Some of these sets may be very old, and their age may be roughly gauged as follows: a fully-finished set averages from ten to fifteen feet below the surface entrance, at a fairly steep angle, and may cover an area of several hundred square feet.

Above the main underground hollow or living-room there can be several interconnecting galleries and a bolt-hole some distance from the main entry. Consequently, a large pile of earth stands outside that entry when a new set is made. But in the course of the years it gets flattened down. Weeds start growing on it, grass as well and once old Kayleg Propert (our scytheman when I was a child) showed me a set which he vowed was over forty years old. What had once been a sizeable pile of earth had been worn down to less than a foot high, and was covered with blackberry. (Kayleg was so-called because on account of his fifty-odd working years as a scytheman he had become knock-kneed on the right leg and when he stood straight his legs made a capital K.)

He was the first person who ever told me that rabbits made use of a badger's set without ever being molested by the owners. Also, that a hunted fox would often make for the nearest badger set, and hide in that, again without being attacked by a badger; and, in my opinion, if it ever came to a fight the badger would win hands down. And the fox, with all those galleries to run about in, could cock a snook when the hunt terriers were sent in to harry him out.

The other morning I was up very early, around 4 am, because I couldn't sleep. I made some tea, and waited for dawn, which comes late at this time of year. However, eventually I could see for twenty or thirty yards and, having opened the front door very quietly, stood there.

Then I heard a noise and knew just what it was because I had heard it before in exactly the same place. It was a badger, hunting around in Patchy's loose box for any dropped pony-nuts.

I waited, believing that it might be the badger who originally had a set on this farm about fifty yards down from the cottage. That was not surprising as the house had only been inhabited very occasionally in the last twenty-odd years. But when we bought it many repairs and alterations had to be done, and for two years we had men working in the house. The badgers decided it was time to depart.

Now, with a little luck, I might get an idea of where they were living now.

In due course the badger waddled out of the loose box door-way, crossed the concrete forecourt and toddled away down the hill to our east boundary fence. I let him get away as he was travelling in a straight line, saw him over our boundary wall and set off along the same trail. At the wall, plain to be seen, were his tracks.

On the other side he had knocked the dew off the long grass and so it was still easy. Then I was lucky. Coming to a small rise, I saw him on the other side. He went down the hill and vanished into the undergrowth.

I followed, and there, on the other side of the thicket, was a fresh pile of earth, with an entry hole inside the thicket. The badger had chosen wisely. Long may he and his descendants live there in peace.

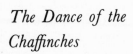
The Dance of the Chaffinches

Here we are in the last two days of September and we haven't yet had the first of the equinoctial gales, due to arrive between 23 September and the end – when we have one – of the Indian Summer.

Well, we did not have one this year and it is time to air our
winter woollies – for those, that is to say, who are still in summer
rig.

But lots of people around here went winter a month ago;
I did, for one.

As to the birds, I have provisioned our drystone wall – not
daily but about bi-weekly, a full six weeks before usual. Three
days ago we saw something else unusual: the close packing on
our power cables of hundreds of chaffinches.

From our nearest post they stretched at least six yards along
each wire, just like swallows getting ready to fly south. I have
never seen so many all at once. Swallows, yes, and occasionally
starlings too. But not chaffinches.

This morning when I went into the stables I saw them again;
not on the wires but in the loose boxes. Serried lines of chaffinches sitting on top of the hay-racks, dozens on the floor busy
gleaning hayseeds and broken bits of cow cornflakes.

Eight or nine were lined up along Rebecca's back but the
little donkey was not bothered. Another three were on Patchy,
but this apparently tickled him – his winter coat is not so thick
as Rebecca's – and every time he shrugged or wriggled his
shoulders they hopped up, coming down again in nearly the
same place as before.

Patchy is a patient beast, although perhaps a bit more sensitive physically than Rebecca. The little dance of his chaffinches
was an amusing thing to watch but I did not want to laugh.
It might have disturbed the birds which, curiously enough, had
taken very little notice of me, darkening the doorway. However,
I had a job to do. I had to put out some hay and a hatful of
corn for each horse.

In this case I actually used my hat to gather a few handfuls
of hayseed off the hay-bay floor for the birds. I put it under
the shelter of the loose boxes so that neither bird nor hayseed
should get over-wet, and taking care not to step on any greedy
bird.

On returning to the house and taking Ann's morning tea up
I mentioned it to her. She said that on the previous day there
had been marsh tits investigating every branch of the forecourt's blackthorns, in case we had filled one of the empty
coconut shells with lard.

We had not, but proceeded to do so after breakfast.

Now, as I write, the chaffinches have begun to disperse, all beautifully be-swollen with hayseeds. There are two marsh tits, four blue tits and a couple of great tits all feeding on fat. We have added two coconuts to our shopping list for later when we go to town.

All this means something. Nature has warned her beasts and birds of something to come and they are all trying to obey her. Our feeling is a bad winter ahead. But what sort of bad? One thing seems to be true. In hill areas, where there is less oxygen and water boils at a few degrees lower than at sea level, we are all more sensitive to the weather.

I guess it is the same all along the fells and dales from Derbyshire, Lancashire and Yorkshire up to Cumbria. We would love to go and find out, but it would take at least three days to get to and from Scholes Farm in Yorkshire, where a great friend of ours lives.

October

Two Swallows Remain Behind

The swallows (all but two) have departed for the Costa del Sol and points further south. The barn owls in the loft are very much in evidence and dying leaves are all over the place.

As to those tardy little swallows, last week there were over fifty sitting in two long lines on the lighting-cables to the house. Then, one day before I got up, away they went.

After breakfast Ann went into the loft and on coming down said that two little swallows had peeped over the edge of one nest and tweeted at her. So they had to be fed in preparation for their long voyage. To collect them and bring them down to the living-room would be a night operation.

It occasionally happens that swallows are left behind and then it is always a question of what to do and how to do it. For swallows do all their feeding on the wing, taking flying insects which on a farm get most of their nourishment off the muck-heap. Whether they are fed to the babies wholesale or partly digested I do not know. In any case feeding a baby swallow is a kill or cure job; but better to kill quickly in warm surroundings than to let it die of cold and hunger on its first flight south to warmer climes.

Shortly after nightfall those two little birds were blinking in the soft light of the living-room, sitting in their nest (we managed to bring it down unbroken) on the edge of the bookcase.

I pounded a handful of minced shin beef with the pestle and mortar and, having reduced it to fibre, moistened it with protogest, an invaluable preparation for reviving newborn lambs that would otherwise die. It comes in little bottles, one lamb-dose, carried by every good shepherd during the lambing in his trouser pocket so it will be warm to pour into the lamb. It is quite a thin liquid but stuffed with protein and revives the most moribund lamb in a few minutes, while the shepherd carries it home to warm up on top of the oven.

I heated the bottle in hot water before using the contents to moisten the fibrous meat-paste. Then I mixed it well, and using a very small medical scoop I put some of this food down the first bird's beak.

Down it went. Likewise with the second. They got the idea and sat side by side with colossal beaks wide open, until each had had four scoopfuls.

Next morning, the second I appeared they jumped to the edge of their nest and sat there, yelling bloody murder until I had warmed the delicious mixture and started to deliver it.

That was three days ago. They are as lively as anything and this morning one of them, while swooping around the living-room, alighted momentarily on Gretchen's head.

The little swallows are very well and now we shall wait for a period of settled weather with, if possible, a clear, sunny day and a good weather forecast over the Continent, when we shall turn them loose. If they fly away to the south they may make it, but if they fly around a bit in futile search for flies then I suppose we are stuck with them until next autumn.

A Crash Landing

The missel-thrush, the largest of his big family, is a permanent resident of Great Britain. His pet name is storm-cock, from his lovable habit of nearly bursting his lungs on the topmost branch of his tree during the most violent of gales. But about here he is scarce.

It was fairly early, with a watery sun briefly visible as it rose over a nearby hill, and I was standing in the middle of the fore-court leaning backward into the wind and looking up at the songster, with his beak wide open, boldly facing the gale and easily outblowing it (for I could clearly hear each note of his song). Then out of the corner of my right eye I saw something like a dingy rag belting by, turning over and over at the mercy of the wind.

It was a seabird of sorts, utterly worn out, travelling at least forty miles an hour and falling fast. Sure enough, about fifty yards further on it struck the trunk of a sapling and fell to the ground.

I went into the hall to put some gumboots on, at the same time putting on my wife's gardening gloves. I've had plenty of experience in rescuing or trying to rescue such casualties. The trouble is that they never know when they are being rescued; to them it seems like an unfair case of brutal assault while incapacitated. Most of them have very sharp beaks which they use continually. Even though this seemed to be a black-headed gull, one of the smaller kinds, I was taking no chances.

I crossed the forecourt, stepped off it and was immediately up to the ankles in mud. I ploughed down to the bird, folded its wings and picked it up with no more than a basilisk glare from its bright and malevolent eyes. I checked each wing for breaks, but there were none there or on its legs. Time would tell whether it was badly damaged or not, but one thing was sure: this time we were lucky. For these black-heads are one variety of the gull tribe that follow the plough. They know all about worms, wire-worms, leather-jackets and suchlike.

In the days of the old horseploughs I have seen two or three gulls actually fighting for a worm between the ploughman's legs, all but tripping him up.

I carried my patient up to the house and put him in the unused henhouse, shutting the door on him while I went for a dig in the muck-heap.

Sure enough there was plenty of treasure, lovely bright worms between four inches and six inches long. These I took and dropped in front of that gull, who had appeared to be moribund not five minutes previously. He ate them as fast as I could drop them and I decided that under the circumstances a complete medical checkup would be quite unnecessary. So I put down a bowl of water and left him there.

When we returned, he was busily searching the north paddock for other delicacies, and he stayed there with us for two days before returning to the seaside.

A Hot Spot for the Owls

A recent gale we had did tremendous damage up here in the hills. Trees fell across various mountain roads and, nearer home, one branch came off the great ash tree nearest the house.

That tree has been sick since the dry summer of 1976, with the top leaves all a-droop each summer since then. For six weeks that year we had to bring our water from the nearest communal pump in the Land Rover; and these great trees in such weather need between one and two thousand gallons a day, according to size. Much though I hate it, we shall have to pollard that tree.

Three or four local inhabitants who really miss that bough are our barn owls and it is funny to see them sallying forth in full flight from our upper granary door for the short seven-yard trip to that bough, to realize just before landing that it isn't there any more. They almost scratch their heads in puzzlement, flying round and round, but it is nowhere to be seen, now cut up into neat logs in the woodshed. They have to go round the corner to the next branch which apparently isn't nearly so convenient.

The barn owls always nest in our north chimney which once served my workroom and the small spare bedroom. I ripped out the workroom fireplace to make room for my safe, and cemented it in. Above the spare room fireplace is a matt of twigs, large and small. In that room we use an electric heater.

We are lucky with owls now. For the last three or four years there have been brown owls (the tu-whit-tu-whoo variety), apparently quite plentiful around here, and they too are welcome. I never have to put poison down for rats, of which there are generally a few around and about; if they get out of hand you are really in trouble and have to call in the county pest officer, at some expense. As to house-mice, our cats are more than capable of looking after them.

Our first bad storm of the year blew itself out and, when it was followed by a flat calm, we realized that winter was here. Last night the temperature was only two degrees above freezing when I made my final round before retiring, with the heavy lamp that gives a powerful beam for at least a hundred yards on a clear night.

I threw up the beam to the living-room chimney, to see whether a wisp of smoke would give the wind-direction if any – and I saw two figures sideways on to me on the stone rim of the chimney.

Two brown owls solemnly turned their head at far more than a right-angle to gaze down at me with huge, brilliant eyes, apparently quite unafraid. Although seeing owls sitting on a chimney may seem strange, it is not uncommon, particularly at the outset of a cold spell, and more so when the fire is wood rather than coal. Not bothered with pollution up here, most farmers use common coal which is cheaper, but much more smoky. However, we always burn wood which makes smoke when wet, but you never get smoke from a dry wood fire, or a dying one.

We let the fire go out when we go to bed, but everything is always nice and warm in the morning, and there is plenty of red ash under the white, too. I reckoned those owls were enjoying a nice cosy temperature of around 26°C. with no nasty coal-smoke to make them cough and sneeze.

How I Saved a Wounded Hare

We were exercising the dogs last week about a mile from the house over a great expanse of open (unfenced) moorland, a marvellous place for riding as long as you know it like the back of your hand. Here and there are deep ditches, overgrown often on both sides by heather, so that you cannot see them unless you know exactly where they are.

Suddenly, about a hundred yards ahead, both dogs stopped abruptly, pointed, crept forward a few yards and disappeared. We hurried on, making heavy weather of it, almost thigh-deep in heather as we were.

Suddenly Gretchen reappeared a few yards away, looking towards us with her most intelligent expression. Almost immediately after, I practically vanished into an invisible ditch about a foot wide and two feet deep. So I walked on along it, soon coming to where Meg was standing over a prone hare in a puddle of blood from a deep slash in its thigh. It had stopped bleeding but had obviously lost a lot.

Too weak to struggle, it made no fight as I settled it as comfortably as possible in the crook of my arm and clambered out of the ditch. We could try to save it but if the worst came to the worst, we could save a bit on the meat bill by jugging it.

Anyhow, when we got home it was still alive and we lay it in front of the fire, with the dogs and one cat as interested spectators. The first thing to do was to lay a small sausage of lint soaked in antiseptic along the gash, both to clean it and keep it damp.

Next, a reviving drink of protogest and, while warming this, I prepared an additional drink of saline mixed with a 5 cc ampoule of sterilized water. Unable to give this in a vein to so small an animal, I mixed it with some of the protein drink and my wife put it down the hare's throat while I sterilized a needle.

Having shaved both sides of the gash and put in four stitches, all was well so far. But as my wife had had no difficulty administering the protein-cum-saline, with the fountain-pen filler, to the extent of about 10 cc, we gave it another dose which would not only put strength into our patient, but would soon get into the circulation to replace lost blood.

We fixed up a nest (or 'form') in a big carton for her – she was a doe – laid her in it and, believe it or not, within ten minutes that little girl was asleep, remaining so for the next couple of hours. We gave her another restorative drink before going to bed that night, and next morning for breakfast she thoroughly enjoyed a couple of lettuce leaves.

By this time she was quite accustomed to us and so, when she started to hop rather gingerly, my wife put a dog-collar on her. We carried her out to a nice patch of grass and put her down. She nosed around a bit but didn't eat any and we concluded that the lettuce had spoiled her. So we took her back and gave her some more with a nice young carrot which she attacked ravenously.

Her wound is healing perfectly – but how she got such a long, deep cut in the first place we shall never know. In a few more days we shall take her back to where we found her and let her go.

The Animals Prepare for Winter

October can sometimes be the most fascinating time of year, and right now it is especially so, though unfortunately a great part of the pre-winter activity cannot be seen due to the still heavy leafage of the hazels that abound in our hedges. This year there was a tremendous crop of nuts and there are still plenty to be seen.

I was walking along a lane to where a neighbour lives, about a mile away, the same place where I once watched a dawn badger destroying and eating the contents of a wasp's nest. Badgers are never about at midday, and on this particular day they were almost certainly fast asleep in their sets. There was plenty of other industrious animal activity to be seen, even in the leafy trees. But one species was noticeably absent: the short-tailed vole.

These very attractive little animals continually sally forth during winter to search, not for nuts or buds, but for the insects they can find sleeping under the bark of trees; easy hunting for active little beasts with very sensitive noses. They seem to lay up no store of food, but are always nice and fat come spring.

Although the hazels are still in leaf, one can spot a nutting squirrel from a hundred yards away or more because of the swaying upper branches. But the approach must be very careful, and even then you may not see anything alive when you get under or near the particular branches you saw waving, because squirrels have wonderful sight and are very wary of human beings. The red squirrel is getting very scarce, and I didn't see any on this walk, although I know that there is one pair with their drey not far from our cottage.

To my astonishment I saw half a dozen long-tailed field-mice, beautiful little things who were busy collecting nuts and beechmast that had fallen – and I wish them luck in this coming winter.

Last of all, in a deep ditch about fifty yards ahead, I saw great animal activity of some sort, and hurried up. It was a very small rabbit, not more than seven inches long, who must have fallen off a foot-high bank into about eight inches of water. He had been over-adventurous and would have paid for it with his tiny life had I not come along.

I scooped him out and gave him several gentle shakes, because naturally he was sopping wet. On I walked, with most of the remaining water draining out of the pocket I had put him in, and when I arrived at our friend's house, I picked him out and deposited him on the fender while my friends put down a saucer of bread and milk.

Such a young rabbit has to be taught to drink out of a saucer, which is easily done by crumbling up some bread in the warm milk, and leaving plenty of the crumbs sticking out of the surface. The smell of cereal is immediately attractive and he starts eating. As he gets a little way down the crumb he finds himself nose-under, and then, lifting his nose clear, starts to lap.

So there I left him, having told my friends just where I had discovered him; they would return him there as soon as he was nice and dry.

A Dormouse Stocks His Larder

Even in summer, when at his liveliest, the dormouse is nocturnal. The most you will ever see is a brief view an hour or so before dawn, or shortly before dark. But the other day I saw one in brilliant sunlight, and very busy he was.

Several times in the last two months I have gently stuck out my neck as various small signs have become apparent which may indicate a hard winter ahead. I sincerely hope I am wrong. But that little dormouse seemed to give me another sign. It was a very warm day for October, with our front door thermometer steady at sixty. There was not a cloud in the sky and the sun was so warm that the horses were lying flat, stretched out fast asleep.

There had been a half-gale the previous night and I was walking past a very thick hazel hedge growing on top of those earthy banks common in these parts.

Under foot the grass was very short and I could see a sprinkling of hazel-nuts. I picked up a few as I went along, finding that eight out of ten were hollow. Having slipped half a dozen into my pocket, I was walking on when I came to a slight bend in the hedge, and around the corner saw a flash of colour. I froze instantly.

I had not been seen. There, not twenty yards away, sat a small furry bundle that instantly betrayed its identity by waving a small thick, reddish tail. It had a head with huge black eyes, large rounded ears, and light-tawny upper parts of the body; it was a fat dormouse.

But by this time of year all adult dormice should be in bed, in the first stage of their long but intermittent hibernation. Occasionally, at long intervals, they awaken, gorge on part of their winter supply, and go back to sleep.

Young dormice on the other hand may stay actively awake until quite late in November, if the weather is mild. Now, this one was huge, positively bursting with fat. Almost certainly, unless a veritable Billy Bunter of a dormouse, this one was an elderly parent dormouse. The way he or she was going about the job indicated this; there was no shilly-shally. Pick up a nut, sniff it, give it a shake, chuck it away. A dud. Try another. Ah, this was a good one! Rapid vanishing act between two large beech tree roots.

This dormouse must already have quite a stock there. So why worry now, so late in the year, about adding to it? Is it possible that he had had some sign from above that this was going to be a shocking winter? Maybe, maybe not. I suppose we shall know by Christmas. In any case, come what may, that little beast should sleep comfy and eat plenty, no matter what the weather.

When he did not return I walked round to see what might be between those roots. The crack went upwards for nearly a foot, and beyond that the tracks of little feet leading even further into the gloom. Quite obviously there was a comfortable dormouse nest up there in the dark beyond – and how many nuts no one will ever know. There he will be safe, even though only a foot above ground level. For the dormouse possesses a very rare gift: he has no scent-glands and therefore leaves no animal scent behind to give him away to any hungry predator like the stoat or weasel.

Four Kites Swoop on their Prey

The other morning I got up at my usual time and to my amazement there was a clear sky in all directions, the first time this had happened for twenty-eight days.

We didn't take long to make up our minds to get out in the fresh air, and less than an hour later had polished off scrambled eggs on toast while Patchy and Blue were getting outside a big feed of crushed oats and hay. As soon as they had finished we groomed and saddled them; then we were on our way.

The previous time we had been out had been an affair of riding-macs and terry towels well tucked in as scarves. This is an old seaman's tip in stormy weather as the towelling sucks up the raindrops and they don't trickle down inside one's clothes, as often happens with a woolly scarf.

Today was utterly different; there wasn't a cloud in the blue sky or a breath of wind. We were high in the mountains and, looking due west, could see our cosy little house with blue woodsmoke coming straight up out of the chimney, with never a curve nor a quiver in it, until it was lost in the sky.

We were riding along a narrow sheep-track which twisted this way and that to avoid the numerous rock outcrops. We were above the timberline but below us stretched a great expanse of conifer forest. And we saw something worth stopping for.

Four kites were circling high in the air, about level with our own eyes in fact, as we were well above them. We were more than half hidden by a huge rock which effectively concealed Blue, my big grey mare. Ann's horse Patchy is a skewbald and she had turned him so that there was but little white showing among the predominant bay.

Two of the kites were somewhat larger than the others, and that meant that this was a pair with youngsters who were being taught to hunt their prey.

It was a fascinating sight and, although kites are very rare hereabouts, you cannot mistake them because of all the hawk family they are the only ones with a forked tail almost like that of the swallow. Then we saw a beautiful sight which I have read about but had never seen.

Suddenly they all stopped dead, as though by a word of command, with tails and wings rigidly outspread, and no perceptible movement.

They remained absolutely stationary for at least thirty seconds. They were over the far side of the forest where we had first seen them, where there was very rough and rocky ground, ideal terrain for rabbit or leveret, although of course we could not see anything as the trees were in the way.

Suddenly, and again as though by command, wings and tails closed as the four birds shot vertically downwards. Almost immediately they were lost to sight. We turned homeward, imagining as we went the sumptuous meal they were probably enjoying.

I suppose in another week or two the parent birds will have had enough of family life. They will have taught the youngsters how to find their prey and the youngsters themselves will by then know exactly what to do and how to eat it.

One day soon the parents will wake up at the crack of dawn and fly away silently, without waking the babies who will then be on their own.

The Night a Bat Came to Call

I have been a countryman all my life but confess that this question of hibernation still has me foxed.

A few days ago I was listening to a television quiz and one of the questions was: 'What animals are true hibernators?'

The answer was the hedgehog, dormouse and bat.

Well, as far as we can make out, the hedgehogs and dormice hereabouts have already gone into winter quarters, as have the bats – or so we thought until a few nights ago.

On this night all went as usual up to this point, but the thermometer was down to only just above freezing.

In any case, the dogs felt the cold, because after about half a minute of their last run of the day they came racing in, blowing great clouds of breath before them. I reckoned that there would be four or five degrees of frost by morning.

I picked up a couple of logs and was just coming in when what should I see but a bat flying rather clumsily around the outside light. There was a large moth also trying to warm itself, and suddenly the bat made a dive at it.

Both hit the glass. The moth fluttered away into the darkness, doubtless cursing a blue streak. The flitter-mouse fluttered to the ground and lay there upside down. Hastily running in to put the logs on the fire, I returned, picked up the bat, taking great care that it could not bite me (for bats' teeth are thoroughly unhygienic) and went inside.

The very warm living-room, with its large open log fire, was quite out of the question, so I took our little visitor to my work-room which, as I hadn't worked in it for a fortnight at least, was nearly as cool as this bat's normal bedroom (the granary over the stables). Having neatly folded him (or her) up in the correct dormant position, and getting the hooks in the right position for hanging upside down, I hung him up on a four-inch nail in one of the beams and left him.

Next morning he was still there and fast asleep. But that evening he was awake and raring to go so, having put on the outside light, I turned him loose. He flew up to the light and waited the coming of the moth.

Since then he has been spending the day in the granary and coming out at night when the outside light is switched on. If he falls again, I shall pick him up, hook him up on a nail in the granary, and hope that he is ready at last for the long winter sleep.

November

The Rabbits who Had Some Fun

On Hallowe'en, or Walpurgisnacht (the eve of 1 May), when witches travel on their broomsticks, nasty things go bump in the night. But we are always all right because this little long-house is surrounded on all sides by countless rowan or mountain ash trees. A healthy little rowan tree even grows out of the north chimney in which the barn owls raise their annual brood.

Planting rowans for good luck was quite customary two hundred and fifty years ago when the house was built. In those days they gave importance to such things.

On Hallowe'en all we have to do is to put a rowan-sprig over each door and window, including barn and stable doors, make the sign of the Cross with a garlic-clove on each and there we are: safe and sound from all that one can't hear or see on normal nights.

On the morning of Hallowe'en, as usual, I was out on the forecourt early getting a smell of the weather. It was a coldish day, windless and no hint of sun. The cats had all come in when I first got down in the dark and now I had left them in the kitchen, getting their usual drink of milk.

Down the front paddock I saw something that I haven't seen anywhere in the Welsh hills since the 1953–4 myxomatosis epidemic. Nowadays if we take a walk over the mountains we are lucky to see three or four rabbits in a ten-mile walk. Yet now I beheld a fascinating sight. There were more than a dozen rabbits, difficult to count because they were having utterly care-less fun. There were three or four does, eight or nine smaller ones, some half-grown, and some month-old youngsters. Presently they calmed down, had a two-minute nibble of short grass and then rushed off again playing leap-frog, ring-a-ring-of-roses and so on, in which even the heavy does were joining.

Some hours later they were still there (the cats were in the kitchen), eating and playing. Could it be that these normally

nocturnal animals were filling up on food and taking their
night's exercise by day because they knew it was Hallowe'en?
So that when night fell they would all be snug in their beds
of bracken and heather on the hillside about fifty yards to the
south?

There, indeed, would they sleep safe from anything that went
bump in the night. For on that small patch grows the thickest
plantation of rowan saplings, from six to eight feet high, that
I have ever seen.

We Put a Kitten on the Mend

We had gone to town to get corn for the horses and it was the
kind of day one would rather stay at home in front of a hot fire.

However, we got the corn on board and headed home.

It was raining torrents, almost like a monsoon rain, and the
water was about six inches deep across the road. We were getting through nice and quiet, like a canal narrowboat, when we
were approached by a van. It flashed past us and a solid body
of water hit our roof and windscreen. Water spurted in from
below as well. Busy Lizzie yelped in dismay. But fortunately,
although the engine must have taken solid water too, Land
Rovers are designed to withstand such insults.

We were thankful that a mile further on there was our Last
Out Inn (which is always our First Inn when we are going shopping) where we and poor little Busy Lizzie could stand in front
of a fire and warm our innards; I was really the worst off as
I had had my right-hand window open.

When we got there and parked, Ann suddenly said that there
was something – a cat perhaps – in trouble. So we all got out
and started looking.

There under a car was a small black-and-white kitten, the
most bedraggled mite I have ever seen, mouth open, yelling
at the top of its voice, blood all down the right side of its face.

It was terrified but we soon caught it, wrapped it in the towel always carried for the windscreen, and took it inside.

In Ann's arms, cocooned in the towel, it soon calmed down and presently the landlady brought a saucer of warm milk, which it lapped very clumsily like a kitten that is still feeding from its mother.

The landlady said she had never seen it around before, but would make enquiries. My first glance at its bleeding eye – obviously a bad scratch from some tom-cat – made me think it might be a dead loss. But once home and nicely cleaned up, it could be seen that the eye would soon heal up with vision probably all right.

Now we have had him for an entire week and he is on the strength of the household. He had cat 'flu, but that is easily cured, after which he will be injected against further attacks as all our other cats are.

The dogs and cats all fell for him, even Thomas the tom-cat, and we are glad of that, because sometimes grown-up tom-cats are beastly to tom-kittens. We have to be careful with the dogs because the big ones, Gretchen and Meg, both weigh over a hundredweight and are heavy in their play. While as to Busy, what she lacks in weight she more than makes up in speed.

Meg has done a Gretchen; she has gone into a false pregnancy and has lashings of milk; but Panda (our name for the kitten) wants none of it; he loves his chopped-up ox-cheek and warm evaporated milk.

So far, no one has claimed a lost kitten. So it looks as if Panda, like Busy, is permanently on the strength.

A Pheasant Follows Me to Safety

I was half a mile from our cottage and about three hundred feet higher up on a bald knob of hill that is unprotected from all the winds that blow except for a small patch of rowan trees, young but thickly self-planted from an older tree now long dead. I wanted to see how their berries had fared after the south-west gale that had roared over the mountains the previous night.

As I got nearer, I could see bare, leafless and berryless branches lifted to the sky. On arriving there a pheasant darted out and hid himself in the heather; a grey squirrel ran away cursing. I saw that the berries were thick on the ground.

From the south-west, on the lightest of breezes, a bank of cloud was slowly drifting up. I could not tell how high it was, because it was lost in the heights of the heavens. But its lower level – well, you could have drawn it with a ruler on a map. Below that level, about a mile away, visibility was crystal-clear. I could see a small bunch of sheep, fifty or sixty, being herded down the mountain by one man and a dog. Above the line was the thick bank of opaque pearly-grey cloud. Within minutes it would reach us.

I waited for it and soon I could see no further than four or five yards.

However, I knew where I was. All I had to do was turn a right-angle left where I was standing, and two hundred yards down the hill is a gate on to a narrow lane, stone-walled on both sides.

I had not gone twenty paces before I heard a low cluck behind. I turned and saw I was being followed by that pheasant! On I went so as not to frighten the stupid thing and on he came again, gently clucking to himself – or could it have been to me?

Pheasants are perhaps the most stupid, defenceless of all wild birds. And here was this one, thinking himself lost in the fog, following me to safety, clucking to himself as cock pheasants will when they are sauntering down a hedgerow with no danger in sight or sound. When they do scent danger it is a different question. They fly upwards like a helicopter and make about as much noise with their wings. Added to that is the deafening clacking they produce from their vocal chords, almost enough to blow off your hat. Now there was nothing but this low, contented clucking, as he carelessly sauntered along exactly three paces behind, in my tracks.

We got to the gate and while I was opening it he slipped between the bottom bars, close enough for me to have touched him. But I did not want to frighten him. In the middle of the road, he stood on tiptoe as he turned left, flapped his wings and clucked quite loudly. I thought he was going to take off, but no, he folded his wings again, and with one departing cluck, started to run quite happily up the road.

I knew his destination, a large patch of conifers about a mile further on. With a wall on either side he could not possibly get lost.

A Wren Hops into our Kitchen

Never in my life, much of it spent studying the habits of the wild animal and bird population, have I known a wren fly voluntarily into a house – until yesterday.

Robins, yes. Often in very cold weather with deep snow, I have known robins dart past anyone opening a house door to get into the warm, following one into the kitchen and impatiently demanding food.

Blue tits, the boldest of all that family, will peck peremptorily on the window, angrily demanding a little attention on the bird-table. If you open the window they will come in and take food off the sill.

Those two naughty but pleasant-in-a-way members of the crow family – jays and jackdaws – have also been known to fly into kitchens in a hard winter asking for food.

But the shy little wren (rightly named the troglodite) shows herself as little as possible, creeping along the branches of the thickest bushes, tucking her nest away in the stone walls that are still common in the hills. And, please God, long may they last.

But this year our annual swallows departed a good month too early for warmer regions because up in the hills the flying insect supply (on which they rely for food) gave out.

This little wren must have come in for the same reason. Her

supply of wren food (also caterpillars, spiders and other small insects) must have been exhausted. For weeks now we have put out coconut shells, either with their own fruit, or filled with hard fat for the tits and also grain for the other birds.

We knew why our wren had come. Every week we get two oxheads and fresh lights for the dogs and cats. This all takes cutting up and there are always small bits and pieces of meat and fat lying about. This wren must have seen the goings-on through the window – but all the windows were shut. How then did she get into the kitchen? For a wren it was perfectly easy.

She hopped in through the ventilator! Impossible? Not at all. Naturally, it wasn't working, but there are exit holes for the draught just one inch square, big enough almost for a wren to fly straight through.

She sat on the chopping-board for many minutes, stuffing herself with tiny morsels of fat. She must have been in the kitchen for at least ten minutes before she was satisfied, pecking busily away and taking no notice of us, who were standing still and quite entranced. Then, having finished, away she went, hopped through the ventilator, and vanished.

But alas, this wouldn't do, for sometimes during the day there are cats in the kitchen. So we blocked up all those draught holes on the outside and that evening put out some more small delicacies on the outside sill of the granary window, under which is the inch-wide hole leading to her trogloditic nest deep inside the stone wall.

Now, morning and evening, we are putting out feed on that sill, because there are two more wrens in that same wall.

*The Crickets Sing
Me to Sleep*

Tradition has it that the cricket is the friend of man, and that goes far beyond Charles Dickens's *The Cricket on the Hearth*, written for Christmas 1845.

Even in those days of the industrial revolution, cottages such as ours were nearly always warmed by an old-fashioned inglenook fire, generally about five feet wide to enable a log to form the major part of the fire.

Our own inglenook was 69 inches wide by 52 inches high from floor-level (that level being a huge flat stone) and 25 inches deep from back to front, with a chimney big enough for a small boy to scramble up and sweep it.

But about 150 years ago the then owners of this cottage went all modern and installed one of the early cast-iron cottage-type stoves which would fit comfortably into any inglenook of the above measurements and were not expensive. When that quality of cast-iron cost one old penny per pound, a range of this sort must have cost something under thirty shillings.

Ours happened to be made and stamped on every panel with the magic word 'Coalbrookdale', one of the first great foundries in this country, opposite Broseley (across the Severn, in Shropshire), and makers of the first iron bridge in the world. The bridge still stands and there is a museum of articles described as 'industrial archaeology', where you may find an iron range just like ours, made any time between 1770 and 1850.

After that date they began to put a water tank on the left side of the fire, with a little brass tap to rack it off. We just have a space where the tank should be, but the fire goes into it and you can boil a kettle or make a very good stew on top of the plate above.

On the left, a separate item really, is a big bread-oven with its own little fire underneath, and this makes the best bread I have ever eaten.

One hundred and fifty years ago this Coalbrookdale bread-unit would have been the latest thing for a small farm and a large family. It was designed to burn wood or peat. We use wood and from cold it will reach 250°C. Thereafter you have to watch it as I imagine it could top 400°C. fairly soon, in one hour after lighting-up. It is unbelievably economical, using only half a wheelbarrow-load of logs a day, and the bread it makes has to be tasted to be believed.

Getting back to the crickets, these friendly little insects were always perfectly at home in the old wide inglenook fires burning peat or wood. It may have been a bit of a jolt when our crickets, around about 1790 or even as recently as 1830, found that lovely little space was being filled with a nasty iron contrivance. But they must soon have realized, cowering under chairs and tables and in corners, that the new ironmongery was still run on peat and wood.

Little by little they ventured forth and discovered something else: the modern brickwork involved had mortar between each brick. It didn't take a diligent and intelligent little cricket very long to discover that he, with the help of a she, could make safe little hidey holes in that mortar.

So it is today. The crickets are still there. Mostly by day they are silent. But at dusk and dawn and all hours in between (at intervals) they can be heard scraping their saw-edged legs up and down to make the chirping noise that is their song.

Three nights ago I couldn't sleep. So I came downstairs, brisked up the fire and sat down in front of it with a long glass of sherry negus, which is said to be good for the sleepless.

As I drank the last of it I heard them singing me to sleep. The fire was warm on my skinny shanks. The negus was warm in my belly.

When I woke up dawn was creeping through the curtains. But a warm little chirping was still coming from the hearth. So I put down some breadcrumbs that I rubbed with a buttery knife for them. Before I dropped off again the chirping had ceased.

The Day We Rescued a Cow

Ann and I were sitting in front of a cheerful log fire in the old range I have described, having our nightcap before going to bed.

Gretchen and Meg were fast asleep on the mat at our feet when there came a thunderous knock on the front door. Gretchen bounded to her feet with a challenging roar and so did Meg.

I went to the door and there stood a friend, John, who has a smallholding a few miles away. He was scarcely recognizable, muddied from head to feet as though he had been dragged through a bog.

'What's amiss?' I asked, and he told me that one of their good cows with a calf at foot, a suckler, was stuck in a bog with the calf. They had managed to get the latter out but the cow was deep in, two men holding her haltered head up.

Their tractor had a flat battery and wouldn't start. Their Land Rover was bogged down over the axles. They knew I had a very good one and always had adequate towing apparatus.

Within ten minutes we were all in our Land Rover with everything that might be needed – a heavy chain, a big coil of rope and a spare battery for the tractor. In a quarter of an hour we arrived at John's little farm and went straight down to the bog where – from a safe distance – the lights of three neighbouring cars were focused on and around the cow.

We backed down as far as I dared to the edge of the bog and John took the heavy-duty battery to his tractor in the barn while Ann and I struggled down to the beleaguered cow.

If this had happened a week previously it would have been all over for cow and calf but, by the grace of God, we had had no rain for a week, and a certain amount of sun.

The mud had stiffened to some extent and I saw that it was stiff enough to shovel away down to her hocks. She was evidently standing on firmish ground, although more than belly-deep in the stiff mud. We could get her out but it would be a ticklish job.

Then we heard John's tractor roaring and then he was there, triumphantly brandishing a roll of tattered carpet.

While the carpet was being cut into strips to lag the rope, two neighbours were shovelling away around the cow's hind legs and the poor beast looked back at us as if to say: That's the idea, chums, but make it snappy; I'm mortal chilled. We were not: for in such emergencies one uses an awful lot of adrenalin.

Within minutes the victim's hind legs had been brought together, wrapped around with carpet, over which went the towing-rope (cut in two) that led to our Land Rover.

Very gently I took the strain, then stopped dead. She had shifted about a foot.

Now came the crunch: someone would have to burrow down

in the mud to get the other rope around her chest behind the shoulders and this was a job I didn't want to do. But I had no time to say so, for a skinny youngster from a neighbouring farm volunteered. 'Ah he's a grand little swimmer,' someone said, and another would-be wag asked him if he'd brought his water-wings. Within minutes that boy had done the job.

The breast-rope was attached to John's tractor and he took the strain, so that both ropes were equally taut. I got into crawler gear, opening the window so that John and I could yell at each other. Away, at about half a mile an hour or less (with no wheels slipping), we went.

Out came that cow, after twenty yards, to lie panting on her side. But with four helpers on either side we soon got her up, and presently (with eight bearers) we got her to a comfortable loose box where her calf bellowed with delight and promptly attacked the nearest tap, which John's wife had thoughtfully wiped clean of mud – and that was that.

Later, after they had been nicely bedded down, we all went to the house, where, in front of a good fire and with the help of some good whisky, we drank to the cow, her calf – and, of course, ourselves.

December

Small Visitors for Breakfast

With the onset of winter various small wild creatures change their habits. Two days ago after a slight snowfall we noticed our tomtit family was congregating.

No longer did they sleep independently. It was very noticeable that they were going round our cottage, inspecting every likely cranny between the stones with which the cottage was built.

They found one. Next morning there was a small pile of age-old mortar on the ground underneath. And in that hole, skilfully enlarged, they'll be able to keep each other warm on the coldest nights, huddled in their safe, warm, communal dormitory. By day they'll feed on what we put out for them: fatty suet.

House sparrows come under a different heading. They get under the eaves and that means they can get inside the house, up in the attic and boxroom section. Heat from the house rises, so they can get the warmth they need on the coldest nights.

The finch family is incredibly tough and the birds are always to be seen at this time of year feeding on hayseeds left by the horses on the forecourt.

Robins too are very hardy little creatures who think nothing of tapping angrily on the living-room window if they think there is anything nice on the breakfast table.

Charity begins, or should begin, at home. The small bird population is one little charity that we should think of because small birds protect our crops and have been disastrously decimated in the last forty years.

Put out a bird-table for them this winter; it will not cost much.

We were discussing this at breakfast when who should tap on the window but a deserving object of charity. Two of them to be exact – a couple of tomtits.

It wasn't a difficult matter to settle. There was plenty of bacon fat on both our plates and a few crusts of toast as well.

Crumbling it up we opened the window and spread it out for them on the sill, but before it had been out a minute there were six more tits, four sparrows, and I don't know how many finches. So I had to go out and watch for our cats until the birds had finished.

How Walking Cat was Injured

As any animal-owner knows, from time to time there can be a big or small tragedy, which with time and patience can be healed.

And, as every animal-owner should know, nature is more to be relied on in many cases than many pills and potions. Nature's first cure with an animal in any case of injury or sickness is rest. Be it what it may, the affected beast leaves the herd or flock, seeks shelter somewhere, and lies down. Sometimes it neither drinks nor eats for any period up to a week.

In the time we have been here there have so far been very few accidents. But the day before yesterday one occurred. It was the day of the garbage run. We are off the main road and the garbage cart cannot get up our lane, so we always take ours to the corner where we turn going down to the village. There it is collected.

We had put the plastic sacks into the back of the Land Rover and I started it up to back out of the garage, on to the forecourt and out through the main gate. Ann was at the gate, holding it open. I had passed Ann and was nearly through the gate when I heard her give an agonized squawk. So I stopped immediately and asked her what was the matter. She said that as I was approaching the gate a rabbit had come rushing up from the down paddock on my blind side hotly followed by Walking Cat, one of the many stable cats. The rabbit had shot at full speed under the car to get into the old garden on my right, which is one mass of very thick cover. Walking Cat, belting after it and still at full speed, had banged into the right front wheel as it was slowly turning in a forward direction, slewed round as though shot and then dashed on apparently unhurt.

She went on to say she had fully feared that we would have one never-to-walk-again Walking Cat. I looked at my watch because the garbage cart comes once a week on the same day and at the same time, and we had only five minutes left. So, as Walking Cat had vanished at full speed, we assumed that she couldn't have been badly hurt, and went on, getting there just in time.

On our return about ten minutes later we found her lying on a piece of foam rubber in the sun. She seemed quite happy and so my wife brought a saucer of milk.

But when she got up to drink, her left hind leg was all wrong, sticking out sideways, and she was walking on the top side of the toes. We felt the leg very gently and it didn't seem to hurt. It was not broken, nor dislocated at the hip so far as we could feel.

From the awkward way she walked, and the fact that she seemed to feel nothing, it was probably nerve damage which might or might not be permanent. Only time would show.

Meanwhile, we carried her inside on her cushion and laid her in front of the range. Almost immediately she tried to jump up to her favourite place on a cold day, on the far side of the range. She just made it on three legs and then fell off.

We put her back on her cushion and there she is still, using nature's remedy: absolute quiet. We have done nothing except to give her a little warm milk from time to time. Obviously there is something badly wrong, but I believe Walking Cat will live to chase more rabbits – because she is taking nature's cure sensibly.

Strangers
in the Night

Three nights ago it snowed for the first time this year and when I got up to shine the torch light out of the bedroom window I saw a thin powdering all over the newly-concreted forecourt.

So far this forecourt has been a mixed blessing; when we let the horses out in early morning they congregate on it and stay there. Why? Because it is the only firm footing on the whole farm, except for the house – and we don't allow horses in the house if we can help it.

A few days ago in a blizzard of hail and sleet from the north I came down to find Patchy and Blue packed like sardines in a can side by side, head to tail (I don't know how they managed that in a space no larger than four by nine feet) in what we like to call the hall. However, there they were and somehow they had even managed to close the front door.

Normally, as is habitual with country people, we never lock either front or back door, night or day, because with two ferocious guard dogs always ensconced on a rug in front of the living-room log fire we always get plenty of warning of visitors.

It only remains for me, correctly attired in a drooping night-cap, to poke a gun out of the bedroom window and quaver: 'This blunderbuss is fully loaded with horseshoe nails and a big charge of best powder', for the nocturnal visitor either to make himself known or to scarper.

Later in the day it snowed again, and I reflected that this, along with the bitter wind, might well bring visitors, other than the horses, seeking shelter from the elements. We have noticed that when you get snow you are also liable to have motorists in trouble, either broken down or with a frozen radiator, or completely lost, asking for help.

That is what happened at two o'clock that morning. We were fast asleep when both dogs started yelling and we heard a call from outside.

I ran down and I was glad to see that there were no horses in the hall. I opened the door and there stood four shivering human beings, man, wife, and a boy and girl, each carrying a small and shivering puppy.

They were lost. They had petrol, oil and anti-freeze in their car, but they hadn't a clue where they were. We are only about four miles from a main road, but they were returning from a visit to mid-Wales and wanted to get to a place in Suffolk not far from Little Thurlow. Once they were on a signposted main road they would be all right, but the question was how to get them on to it?

Meanwhile the wind howled down from the north with an occasional snow flurry. You never know how things are going to turn out up here, so I ushered them into the living-room, having shushed down the guard.

In they came to a room which soon had a bright log fire burning and two colossal dogs interested only in the two pups. We left them for the night to sleep on settees.

Next morning I went down to find them all up and a roaring fire burning. Apparently at about five o'clock Gretchen had poked the husband awake, pointing to the fire and the fact that it was getting very low.

He got the idea almost immediately, rose and fed it with logs, after which Gretchen (and the visitors) went to sleep again.

After a big farmhouse breakfast we got the Land Rover out, saw them into their own car, and piloted them down to the main road with clear instructions how to get back to Suffolk.

An Injured Blackbird

In common with other inhabitants of this country, we have had to draw in our horns and look sadly at every penny we take out of our pockets before putting it back and saying: 'Oh well, we can go without this or that', whatever we were thinking about. But one really worthwhile saving we have been able to indulge in has been to lay up our horseless carriage. There she sits in the garage – unlicensed, uninsured and with no certificate of roadworthiness.

We have horses and we are thus mobile. With one ride to town a week and ample saddlebags (the Spanish *alforjas* or *maletas*) on each saddle, we can bring back an eight-day supply of all the food we need for the price of a ten-mile ride and a few warming drinks (plus an apple or so apiece for the horses) with perfect ease.

Heavy reserves such as meat and tinned food had been built up before laying up the Land Rover, because in a situation like ours it is always wise to have at least six weeks' supply of everything you may need for man and beast in case of prolonged snow at this time of year. We even have about four tons of dry logs stored under cover in one of the loose boxes and plenty of paraffin for lamps and heating in case of a mains failure.

The other day we were returning from our shopping trip at an easy jog along our single-track road when, on a double hairpin bend, we came across a prone blackbird in the middle of the track.

As we approached, it struggled and fluttered to get to the hedge, obviously not knowing that no horse will willingly put a foot on any living thing – except perhaps an iron-shod hoof on the toes of its owner just for fun. Our horses, seeing the invalid, obligingly stopped (without any signs from us) a foot short of it.

I jumped down but not so quickly (encumbered as I was with thick gauntlet gloves and my heavy old Army greatcoat) as Ann. While I was still blundering about, she jumped down, neatly caught the bird and put it into an empty space on one side of her saddlebags.

On we went to finish the remaining couple of miles between us and the warm living-room with Ann telling me the bird had a leg broken below the 'knee' and one wing possibly broken.

Once home, Ann measured out the corn and pony-nut ration for the horses while I chucked a couple of logs on the fire and had a look at the bird. The leg was broken half-way down from the 'knee' and, as it was an old bird, I removed the lower half by cutting the bit of skin remaining. The leg of nearly all birds below what we call the 'knee' is pretty insensitive, and in this bird very much so.

The wing, thank goodness, was neither broken nor dislocated but probably sprained. Nasty enough but not fatal. The smaller the bird the more difficult these tiny bones are to set or, in the case of a dislocation, to reduce. In such cases a speedy dismissal to the birds' paradise is the merciful course.

However, having disinfected the stump, I put an elastic band round the wings and carefully set it up on its remaining foot in a cardboard box.

When Ann returned she sent me out to dig for worms in the muck-heap and while I was doing that she put down a little warm water with added protein. The bird had managed to drink quite neatly, standing sturdily on one leg and, when I returned with half a cupful of small red worms, had a field-day among them.

In another three days we shall be able to return it whence it came so that it will find its mate, to which they appear to remain steadfast. We have six blackbirds up here round the house, always in pairs, one black and one dark brown.

Christmas Dinner for the Birds

It looks as though we shall have everyone's wish for a white Christmas answered. We already have it white all over the mountain tops (and our own little place as well), not with snow but with frost. For the last three nights we have had a constant night temperature of $-7°C$., never above freezing in the day-time. If we get snow, the first few flakes will stick and it will then build up fast.

One point that always impresses us is the winter coat of Rebecca our donkey. Her hair is so long and so thick that it almost looks the coat of an Angora goat, but a bit more straggly. Patchy has a more than usually thick coat and almost every day takes a roll in the mud, because it dries on quickly and is added protection against deep cold.

In this weather life is terrible for small birds. We have an enormous following at the moment, not so much because there are many birds nowadays but because within a five-mile radius there are several abandoned farms. The birds that used to live round them have come to us. Even in the bird world there is a bush-telegraph.

We buy our bird food by the 28-lb sack, which is economical when helped out by household scraps.

When our drystone wall is bare, the birds know what to do. Bravest are the tits, then the robins, closely followed by the chaffinches. They come and tap on the window even if three or four cats are glaring or yowling at them from the other side of the glass. Fair enough on the birds, but a dirty trick on the cats.

We have had to make other arrangements for the cats. While the weather is like this they have to stay in the house from 7.30 am to 4 pm, by which time it is nearly dark, bitter cold and the birds are seeking their sleeping-quarters. So we fixed up our back-alley as the cats' day-nursery.

Three feet wide and five feet long with a good door at each end and a very low roof, it is ideal for them, dry and draught-proof. For warmth in this weather they have one of those old-fashioned paraffin burners we used to put under the engine of our horseless carriage in the days before anti-freeze was invented. The burner is utterly reliable. The cats cannot tip it over and it is nice to see them all sitting round it in their nursery, which has a big window, too, but no view of a bird-table. If they want to sleep, there are deep cardboard boxes for them. There is even a sprig of holly there. So it looks Christmassy as well as warm and comfy.

Meanwhile, there are three great tits, four tomtits and two marsh tits tapping away on the living-room window, while I write – this room being warmer than my workroom.

I look out the window. Two coconut shells (four halves, that is) still have plenty of nut in them, but three half-shells that contained melted fat set hard (so it won't tumble out) are perfectly empty. Ann knows this as well as they do and has three more ready. Five minutes later she is out there, hanging them up, and the tits have left my window. Indeed, one is on her hand, one is on top of her head and another on her shoulder.

Every Christmas we seem to get stuck into Dickens, either the story of Scrooge and Tiny Tim or the Christmas celebrations for Mr Pickwick and his friends at old Wardle's farm Dingley Dell. There is but little to choose between them save the picture of the goings-on in the Dingley Dell kitchen by my favourite artist Phiz.

This was the old-time Christmas. There is no Christmas tree in the kitchen because that custom would not be brought in until the young Queen Victoria married Prince Albert. He imported the German Christmas, with Santa Claus, the holly tree – and what we know as the modern Christmas card – to Britain.

In the Dingley Dell kitchen there is a huge log burning bright in a wide inglenook, in front of which stands old Wardle and several cronies, but not blocking the heat because it seems to light up the whole room. There are garlands of evergreen hanging from the beams in close contact with hams and a flitch or two of bacon. Mostly holly, of course, but quite probably some of the ripe red berries are of mountain ash. In the middle of it all is a vast branch of mistletoe hanging low, under which Mr Pickwick is gallantly kissing Mr Wardle's mother, a sometimes acid old dame who is at times – like myself – conveniently deaf.

There isn't a Christmas card to be seen because there were as yet no railways and it would have been unthinkable to load stage coaches with them.

Christmas is coming, the goose is getting fat,
Please to put a penny in the old man's hat.
If you haven't got a penny a ha'penny will do,
And if you lack a ha'penny, a farthing will do.
But if you haven't anything, well, God bless you.

We used to recite that old jingle at Christmas time in the old days when farm workers were getting around a pound a week. But one thing they seldom suffered from was rheumatism. With good leather boots available at about five shillings a pair and good leather gaiters for less than that, they never laid up a store of rheumatism or arthritis.

I was thinking on these things as we set up our Christmas tree, wondering whether we should have reverted to the older style of holly garland, mistletoe and a great yule log in our inglenook, because as soon as there are glass bobbles hanging from the branches of a four-foot tree on the table, I am afraid the cats would fight to see who could climb it first.

I needn't have worried. The cats behaved themselves perfectly, looking at the tree with disdainful eyes. After all, they seemed to say, there are bigger trees outside and we've learned to climb them all.

But Meg thought differently. In addition, there was a thing on top (our angel) that was much the same colour as the brand of chocolate drops which I hand out to them every night before going to bed.

My wife and I were in the kitchen inspecting the free range turkey which is just small enough to go into the bread-oven. Suddenly there was a crash. We rushed in and there was Meg, astride the now prone tree, inspecting the angel and slobbering. We righted everything, telling Meg (who weighs one hundredweight) that it was no question of doggie chocs but a real Christmas tree angel.

She was not convinced I was right until I produced the real chocolates and gave her and Gretchen a handful apiece. Then I left the tin in full sight on the end of the bookshelf so that they would know.

As we finished decorating the tree we could hear the faint sound of carol singers practising away four miles down the valley.